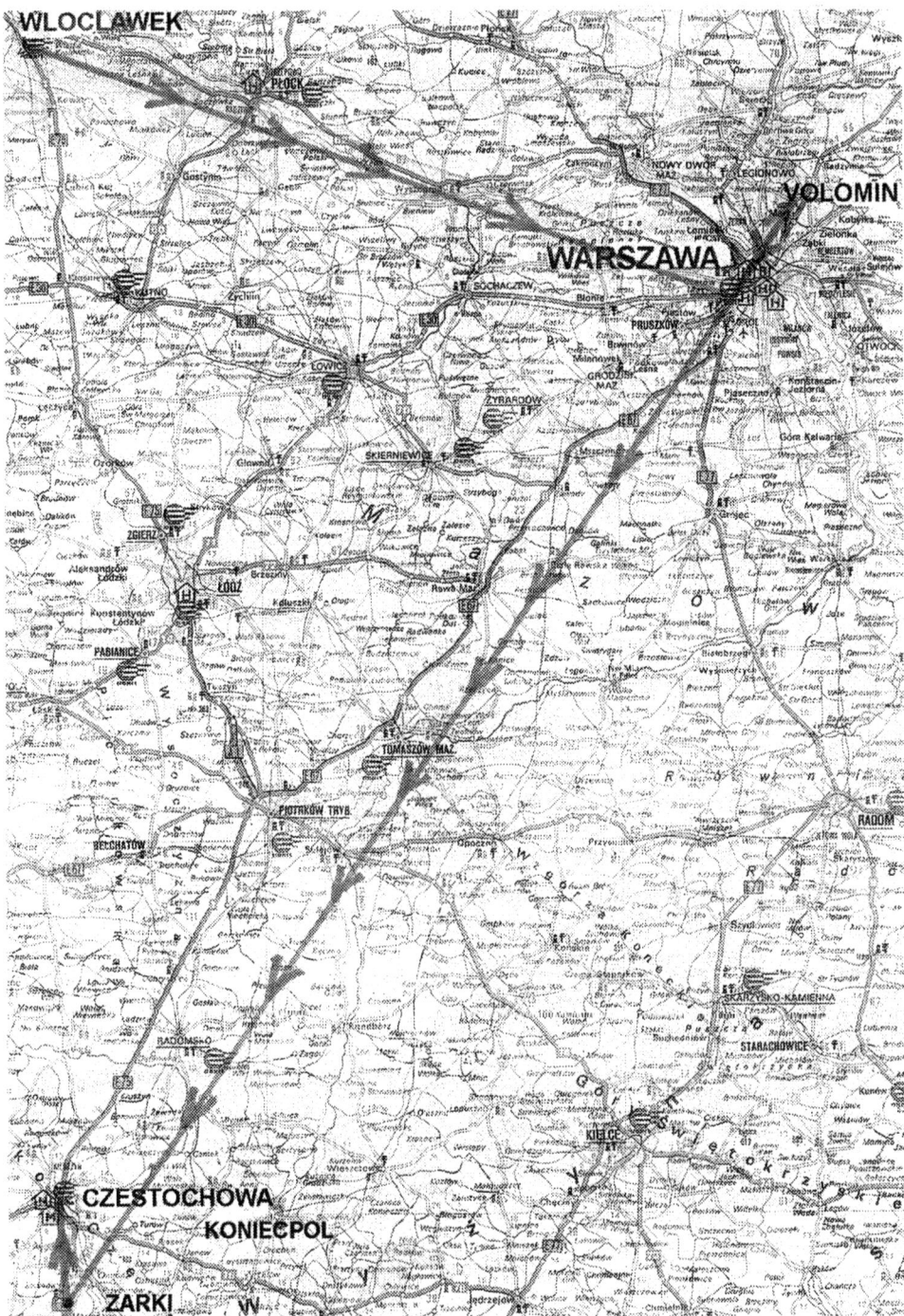

Partial Map of Poland showing Peninah's route

Flight to Survival

Wloclawek – Warszawa
Czestochowa...Eretz-Yisrael
1939 to 1945

A personal narrative

Peninah Cypkewicz-Rosin

Flight to Survival

Wloclawek – Warszawa
Czestochowa…Eretz-Yisrael
1939 to 1945

Copyright 2006 by Peninah Cypkewicz-Rosin and Josef Rosin
All rights reserved
First Printing: May 2006, Iyar 5766.

Translation from the Hebrew: Sarah and Mordehai Kopfstein, and Josef Rosin

Text Editor: Nancy Lefkowitz;

Layout: Joel Alpert;

Cover Design: Adina Alpert

JewishGen, Inc
2951 Marina Bay Drive Ste 130-472
League City, TX 77573

Printed in the United States of America by Lightning Source, Inc.

Library of Congress Control Number (LCCN): 20069218
ISBN: 0-9764759-9-5 (hard cover: 195 pages, alk. paper)

Remarks:

All Yiddish and Hebrew names are transliterated according to the rules issued by YIVO.

Because of the technical difficulties the Polish town names and places are printed without the special Polish letters and symbols, but instead the closest Latin letters are used.

We note in particular that the Polish towns of *Czestochowa* and *Wloclawek* would be transliterated as *Chenstochova* and *Vlotslavek* respectively.

Others towns are:

Polish	English Transliteration
Lodz	Loodz
Dobrzyn	Dobzhin
Milecin	Milenchin

This true-life story is dedicated to the
memory of my beloved parents:

Leizer (Eliezer) Cypkewicz
and
Gucha (Gitl) nee Rubinstein

To my dear children Ami and Eliyah, I wrote these memoirs for you and for my grandchildren Sharon, Gil, Inbar and Lior. I wanted you to know about my family, your grandfather and your grandmother, as well as my experiences during the war and for some time thereafter.

To my nephew Naor and niece Niva I hope that you too will find my life story of interest. It includes the history of your father Shemuel-Leon, my brother, and will familiarize you with our parents, your grandparents.

To Hanah, my sister-in-law, when your grandchildren search for their roots, they will find them in this book.

To Irith, Tsevika, Vered and Yits'hak, I would be pleased if you, the spouses would also read this book.

With love to all of you,
Peninah

Preface and Acknowledgement

I originally wrote these memoirs in 1996 in order to tell my children and my late brother's children about the family in which I grew up, about their grandparents, and about the events my brother and I experienced during the war and for some time thereafter.

I would like to thank the following people, without whom this memoir would never have seen the light of day:
My husband, Josef Rosin who was instrumental in persuading me to write about these painful memories. Without his encouragement I doubt if I would have ever been able to record them. He was a great help in organizing the chapters in which I tell the story.

I also want to thank all the following friends and family who contributed greatly to the telling of this story: Aryeh Gutkind, Rachel Tratsevitsky-Beker and Pola Lubling-Rapaport who helped refresh my memory; Sarah and Mordehai Kopfstein for their incomparable help to my husband in translating this book from Hebrew into English; Nancy Lefkowitz for her careful editing of the English material and Fran Senner Hurley for her fastidious review of the text; Joel Alpert who worked with Carol Skydell of JewishGen on the publishing aspect and for the book layout; and Adina Alpert for the design of the cover.

I have attempted to adhere to the facts as faithfully as possible and to this end, I was assisted by the *Memorial Book of Wloclawek and Vicinity* (Hebrew and Yiddish), Published by The Association of Former Wloclawek Jews in Israel and in America, Israel 1967 and by *The Memorial Book of Czenstochowa*, Volume 2, published by Encyclopedia of Diasporas, Jerusalem. 1968.

P. C.- R.

Table of Contents

Chapter 1: Wloclawek
Wloclawek -- My Hometown

Wloclawek was my hometown and where I grew up. I loved the place and thought then that it was the most beautiful town in the world. It was a pleasant town with lots of green landscapes and surrounded by woods. It is situated on either side of the Wisla River. The town developed mostly on the left bank, where the majority of the Jews lived, including my family and me.

The old wooden bridge on the Wisla River

Along the river there was, and still exists, a beautiful promenade with many chestnut trees that I was able to see from a window in our flat. I especially liked looking at one of those trees and its branches. In my imagination it changed into different shapes and scenes. Those imaginary figures and scenes are still in my memories. When I visited Wloclawek in 1994 for the first time after more than 50 years, among the beloved things I looked for and found, was that tree still standing there.

Along the promenade there were benches and at the end there was a podium where the Polish Army band of the fourteenth regiment performed on Sundays during the summer. We children used to run there to listen to the music, which were mostly marches. We also enjoyed looking at the soldiers, and gossiping among ourselves. On the way we used to buy *beigls* at one of the many kiosks that were scattered along the promenade. These bagels had been threaded onto a string and formed a chain.

My Fantasy Tree (1994)

The promenade along the Wisla River (1994)

Third of May Street

Above is a picture of the pleasant Third of May Street stretching from Liberty Square to the Old Market. As children and teenagers we used to walk back and forth along it to be seen and to meet friends.

The Old Market Square

Below is the magnificent Sienkiewicz Park, named after the famous Polish writer. The park was divided into three parts by a little stream (Zglowiaczka) that flowed through it. Each part was connected to the others by small arc shaped bridges. In each section there were different flowering plants and trees and lilac shrubs with their beautiful fragrance. In the autumn I watched the leaves change into splendid colors before they fell to the ground. Near the little stream there were pleasant corners with beautiful flowers and benches where I often sat with a book in my hand while the sound of the swirling water in the background always brought on feelings of peace and tranquility.

A typical winter scene in Sienkiewicz Park

As I recall there was a big plot in town at Kaliska Street. In summer it was a place to learn to ride bicycles, and to ice-skate in the winter. I owned skates and I loved to skate to the sound of music with the cold air blowing in my face. We also sledded down the sloping Brovarna Street from the top to the very bottom of the street.

Wloclawek was a medium sized town with not a particularly large Jewish community. In 1931 there were 56,000 residents with about 10,000 or 18% who were Jews. Nevertheless, the Jews in town were very active and they had established all of the institutions that contribute to a thriving community. A democratically elected committee administered all community matters. All the different factions in the community were represented, but it was the Zionist organization that had the greatest influence. The operating income for the committee came from taxes, donations and inheritances. Most of the money was spent on the upkeep and maintenance of the Jewish Hospital, the Home for the Aged and the Orphans Home. There was also a budget for culture and education as well as funds to help children from poor homes.

There were two synagogues in the town. The old one was on Zabia Street and the new one on Krulewiecka Street. There were a few libraries with many books in Polish, Yiddish and Hebrew. There were also a few sports clubs with *Maccabi* at the head. Their hall served as the cultural center for the local Zionist organization. There was an amateur theater group (*Di Yiddishe Bine*) whose shows were high quality and famous in the town and surrounding area. My father was one of its central pillars. All Zionist parties were represented, including the *Bund*[1] and even the illegal Communist Party that functioned underground. Most of the Zionist youth organizations were active in town, which added to the social life for the young people. The most prominent was the *Hashomer-HaTsair* that had about 590 members in 1939.

During the years when Poland was independent (1918-1939), most of the Jews in Wloclawek made a living from light industry, crafts and commerce. However, during the years just before the war some liberal professionals arrived in the community. This was the Wloclawek I loved, but there was another Wloclawek

---

[1] Bund - A Jewish anti-Zionist socialist workers organization

too. This was the town of Polish anti-Semites who plotted against Jewish youth and called them names and sometimes even fought with them. During the years before the war the situation became worse and anti-Semitic students circulated proclamations in which they called for a boycott of Jewish merchants and artisans. They even stationed students in front of Jewish shops to prevent buyers from entering which had a significant impact on the lives of the Jewish population. To be truthful I should point out that not all Poles were like these. There were also others who came to help and once even prevented a pogrom.

Father's Side of the Family

When I started to write about my family I realized how little I knew about it. I regretted this very much and it was hard for me to understand why I had not been interested in my ancestors. Was it due to my youth? Was I just too busy with my own interests and needs? Perhaps it was because I accepted Father and Mother and their families as a fact that existed when I became a part of it, expecting that it would exist forever? For this story I have tried my best to recall as many of the events in my life as possible.

I did not know my paternal grandfather as he passed away before I was born. I don't remember if I was ever told anything about him either. I presume that his name was Shemuel because all my uncles had sons called Shemuel, and this was also my brother's name.

My paternal grandmother was the only daughter of her parents. She was a lovely woman with a pleasant voice, but she had some kind of eye disease. In the process of trying to cure this defect she became blind. She always prided herself that in spite of being blind, she found a husband and bore him four sons. Two of them had the family name Cypkewicz and the other two, Mintz. I don't know how that happened. Maybe it was related to avoiding service in the Czar's army. (When they were born, Poland was part of the Russian empire). Grandma was also proud of the fact that during World War I she was able to smuggle food and other items across the border since the soldiers never stopped her due to her blindness. After Grandpa's death, Grandma moved to her son's home in the small town of Wolomin 20 kilometers (12 miles) northeast of Warsaw. A few years later she came to live with us in Wloclawek. We loved her very much and my brother Shemuel was particularly close to her. I remember once when Grandma put on her coat intending to go to a doctor Shemuel thought that she was leaving us. He tugged on her coat and would not let her go until she promised that she would come back. She told us tales in her poor Polish or in Yiddish before we went to sleep. Despite the fact that we did not understand everything, we enjoyed her story telling very much. She also sang Yiddish folksongs to us and sometimes it was very amusing when she held a book upside down and pretended that she was reading a story to us. She stayed with us until she died at the age of 83 at the second *Seder of Pesakh* in 1939. She was ill for only two days and on the second day of her illness she suddenly sat up and said: "Children, they have come to take me." She was lucky to reach that age and to pass away before the Nazi invasion.

Grandmother had four sons. My father Leizer (Eliezer) was the firstborn. The second was Shelomoh, the third was Mordehai who lived in Wolomin and the youngest was Alter. Three of grandmother's children lived in Wloclawek, married and had children. Uncle Shelomoh and his wife Pesia (who was my mother's sister) had two sons and a daughter. The firstborn was Reuven, the daughter Perl-Pola was nearly my age, and the son Shemuel-Shmulek was close in age to my brother. When we were children we often played together, but when we grew up we grew apart. Cousin Perl joined the *Beitar* [2] organization. My brother and I joined *Hashomer HaTsair*[3]. During the war she joined the

---

[2] Beitar - The Zionist youth organization of the Revisionist Party
[3] Hashomer-Hatsair - A leftist Zionist youth organization

Polish underground, (she looked like a Polish girl) and she was killed apparently in battle, although I have no proof of this. Cousin Shmulek survived the Holocaust, but was murdered by Poles afterwards. I do not know under what circumstances. People told me that he had been encouraged to join the *Olim* (immigrants) to *Eretz-Yisrael,* but he preferred to stay with the Polish woman who apparently hid him during the war. Nobody survived from this family.

My Father Leizer (Eliezer)

Uncle Shelomoh made a living by producing school bags that he sold to shops. Uncle Alter married a few years before the war and had a little girl. He survived the Holocaust and returned to Wloclawek where my brother who had returned from Russia, met him. I corresponded with him for some time, but we too grew apart. I don't remember why. Maybe it was because of the War of Independence in *Eretz-Yisrael* or because he and his second wife left to live in France where his wife had relatives. Regardless, the connection was never resumed and I am very sorry about it. When he had written he told me what happened to him during the war when he and his family were among the first ones the Germans sent from Wloclawek to Ozerow.

At Treblinka there is a stone in memory of the Jewish community of Wolomin

Some time later my mother came to them from Warsaw, and they managed to live together. One day the Germans seized Uncle Alter in the street and he was sent to a labor camp in Czechoslovakia. After the war he heard that the Germans had sent all the Jews who lived in Ozerow to the death camp in Maidanek and among them, apparently, were his family and my mother.

Uncle Alter 1947

My uncle Mordehai from Wolomin, was married to Hadassah. They had five children, four daughters and one son, but I don't remember all their names. I had stayed with them during the war for a few weeks. I do remember Bronka the eldest daughter very well because she sometimes joined us on our vacation trips to Milenchin a village about four kilometers (2.5 miles) from Wloclawek. A short time before the war her parents arranged a marriage for her to a man she did not want to marry. She was a tall blonde beautiful girl, whereas the groom was short and not very good-looking. Despite not wanting to marry him she consented. Apparently they had no dowry for her, and there were three more daughters in the house. My uncle was a trade agent with probably a very modest income. When the war began, Bronka and her new husband managed to escape to Russia. They were there for a while, but she left him and returned to her parents in Poland. The uncle was also blonde and looked like a gentile so during the war, when Jews were already forbidden to travel by train, he was able to take the train to Warsaw and do business with the Poles. I can only assume that his whole family perished.

Mother's Side of the Family

I was able to get to know Grandpa Rubinstein on my mother's side when I was quite grown up. He lived in Warsaw and I think owned a bakery. His daughters were angry with him for many years because of his attitude toward them after their mother's death. He married another woman who people said behaved like the proverbial cruel stepmother. To my regret I don't know how old the girls were when their mother died, and I also don't know whether they stayed with their father and stepmother, or whether they were already grown and able to care for themselves. I don't even know whether they were born in Warsaw, because Mother told me once that as a girl she lived in Ostrowitz. When I was about 8-10 years old, Mother reconciled with her father and she took Shemuel, my brother, and me to meet Grandpa. I remember that he spoke to us, asked all kinds of questions and at the end said that we were smart children. I cannot remember how he looked or his name. This was the only time we saw him. He died shortly after this visit.

Grandma's name was Perl, and all my cousins from Mother's side and I were named after her. The grandparents had four daughters and one son who was the firstborn. I don't remember his name, but I do remember well his visiting us from Warsaw where he lived. He left quite an impression on me. I was a small girl, and he was describing his trip to Venice, the town built on water. I was quite hypnotized and from then on dreamt of seeing this wonderful town of Venice one day. Many years later this strong wish ended with an involuntary immersion into the Grand Canal. This uncle was married and had a girl named Perl, of course.

My mother Gitl-Gucha had three sisters and one brother. Their names in order of their ages were Pesia, Malkah and Hayah. Mother was the eldest. I already described Pesia and her children, because her husband was Shelomoh, my father's brother. I have no idea how the match between them was arranged. Malkah lived in Warsaw with her husband and if I am not mistaken, they had two boys. They had a small factory that produced candies and marmalade. When mother went to Warsaw she always returned with a great supply of sweets. The youngest sister Hayah was a beautiful brunette and a very nice person. She lived in Warsaw and had a boyfriend who was a communist and often was jailed. The family disapproved of this match and she did not marry until the age of 32. Eventually she came to Wloclawek and it seems to me that my parents arranged her marriage to a man a few years younger than herself. They married and stayed in Wloclawek where they had a little girl named Perl, of course. All perished in the Holocaust.

My Parents

Mother was a lovely woman and as a girl she was called the beautiful Gucha. She was blonde with blue eyes. She was a housewife without any special skills, but when needed, helped a little in the family's cardboard box factory, mostly sending the boxes to the clients. She accompanied Father to all his social activities.

They went out frequently in the evenings and Grandma stayed at home with us. Mother was very devoted, a real Jewish mother, who worried especially about her children. It seems to me that I inherited this characteristic from her. When one of us was ill she would spend a lot of time playing games with us or making different kinds of wonderful paper figures. To her credit, I must say that she never prevented us from participating in the activities customary among the children and the youth. We only had to promise her that we would be careful and come home on time. Nevertheless, all the warnings I heard from her made me fear many things. I did not learn to swim because of the fear of drowning, nor did I excel in ice-skating because of the fear of falling and breaking my neck. My brother Shemuel was less influenced by Mother's fears. He learned to swim, and quite quickly ice-skated well. Once when Mother and I saw him paddling a kayak on the Wisla Mother almost fainted. We didn't go home until we saw him come back safe and sound. At first I was afraid to enter the ice skating rink, but Shemuel took my hand and steered me to the middle of the rink and said: " Now you skate by yourself." I had no choice and started to skate. When I went to *Hashomer-HaTsair* at the age of 14, Mother asked me to return home at 10 PM. It was very inconvenient, because sometimes I had to leave in middle of an activity or a lecture and go home by myself. After some time I convinced her that it was safer for me to go home together with my friends after the activity rather then run home by myself at 10 PM at night

In our house there was a concierge who at 10 PM, and sometimes even earlier, locked the gate and went to bed. When I returned home after 10 PM, I had to ring and wait for the concierge to wake up and open the gate for me. Sometimes it took quite a while and it was unpleasant to wait in the street. Therefore, after the activities in *Hashomer–HaTsair* the boys escorted most of the girls home. Mother was satisfied with this arrangement, but less satisfied when the escorts were Polish boys. Not long ago a friend from the youth movement, Lutek Tabachinsky, whom I met at the Memorial Meetings for Wloclawek Jewry, reminded me that that one boy escorted me home and gave the concierge 20 *Groshen*. Mother was satisfied with this arrangement, but less satisfied when the escorts were Polish boys.

Once, when I was already studying at the Polish evening school, Mother saw me outside our house accompanied by two Polish boys. How she knew that they were Polish was a puzzle to me. She remarked to me that she would not like to have a *goy* for a son-in-law in spite of the fact that I was very far from thinking about marriage at all. I think that this remark was made because our neighbors' daughter married a Polish boy. They lived one floor below us. The woman was a widow, still young and good looking, with two nice blonde girls. The elder one was 19 to 20 years old and married a Polish boy in a church. This resulted in a great tumult among the Jews in town. As a little girl I used to play with Polish children who were neighbors from across the street, and Mother did not object.

Mother was practical, but Father wasn't. He was easily liked by others, and a man who impressed people by his appearance. He was always willing to help others. For example, he posted bail for someone and later on was forced to pay the debt instead of the person owing the money. This made Mother angry. We were not rich, but my parents made a decent living. I can't recall a case when we children asked for something that we were denied. My friends knew that Father would give me money if I asked, whether it was money for the youth movement or for other purposes. He was an active person and his main occupation, except for earning a living, was the Jewish theater (*Yiddishe Bine*), which was established in the town in 1927. He was one of its central pillars.

This was an amateur theater with the goal of raising the cultural level of the Jewish population in town by presenting excellent and artistic plays. It resisted putting on anything deemed not worthy. The theater company also performed in the small towns around Wloclawek, especially on *Hol Hamoed* of *Pesakh* and *Sukkoth*. Actually the plays had a beneficial effect on Jewish youth. Mother always joined Father on his trips even just outside of town.

This theater was Father's greatest love outside of family. He devoted himself to it wholeheartedly and sometimes it not only cost him a lot of time, but also money. The theater presented plays from the best Yiddish repertoire. Father acted in most of the leading roles and sometimes directed them. Many people remembered his performances in the dramatic roles as Hone the Gravedigger in *The Treasure* by David Pinsky, as Tevye in *Tevye the Milkman* by Shalom-Aleikhem and in many other plays. He directed the plays *Yizkor* by H. Sekeler, *The Voice of Blood* by

J.D. Berkovitz, and *The Miracle of Perl* by Shalom Ash. There were many more as well. He also gave evening performances in the small surrounding towns.

Below is a piece written by Leml Lichtenstein, one of the members of the theater, taken from the Wloclawek Memorial Book. He managed to come to *Eretz-Yisrael* a short time before the war. He wrote: "Grushka[4] (Cypkewicz), but we called him *Dziadek* (Grandpa in Polish), not because he was the eldest among us, but because of his warmth and friendliness to everyone regardless of their importance. The theater was like a holy place for him and he adored the great players. He was very active and participated wholeheartedly. On the day of a premiere he would not leave the stage and cared for everything. Furthermore, he was a popular man and a good friend to everybody who was able to get in touch with him and therefore he was loved by everyone."

Our life at home was also influenced more or less by the theater. I recall the excitement at home before each performance and especially before a premiere. Father used to leave the house in the morning for the performances taking place on Saturday evenings. Mother, Shemuel and I, came to the hall before lunch to see the rehearsals and the final arrangements before the show. The sets were arranged, the actors were rehearsing their roles and everybody was a little excited and nervous. The atmosphere hypnotized me. In the evening Mother would take me to the show. I was 10 or 11 years old and Shemuel, who was younger than I, would stay at home with Grandma. When he was older he would join us at the plays. We would come a few hours before the show and look around behind the curtains to see how the actors made up and dressed, suddenly becoming different figures greatly stirring our imagination.

---

[4] Grushka - Some people called him so and I never asked him about it

Di Yiddishe Bine - the theater group on their way to perform outside Wloclawek, 1930. Standing third from left-Father, sitting-Leml Likhtenshtein, in the bus third from left-Mother

Mother (left) and Father

(Enlargement from the picture above)

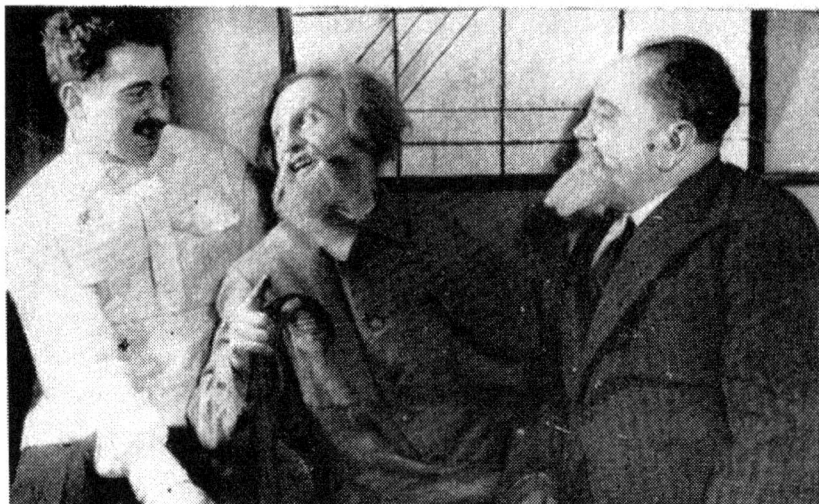

At the play *Life is Calling* by Bielotserkovsky
From left: L. Likhtenshtein, Hozenfeld and Father

At the play *The Country Boy* by Osip Dimov (1923)
From left: Henia Alpert, Father, Rafael Radzievsky,
L . Likhtenshtein.

Sometimes I would look through the hole in the curtain often used by the actors so they could see what was going on in the hall and to get an idea of the type of audience that night. Usually the halls were full since the Jews in Wloclawek hungered for theater. The Yiddish stage was at a high level so that even Jews, who thought of themselves as Polish in every way, used to attend these performances.

Shortly before the beginning of the show we would go down into the hall, sit in the first row of course, and the show would start. Now it looked different again. With everything in its place the lighting added different effects and the story unfolded. To be honest, I did not always understand the essence of the plays, either because I did not know enough Yiddish or because I was too young. Actually it didn't really matter because I was fascinated by the activity on the stage in this world of make-believe. After the show we would go backstage to wait for Father who had to remove his makeup. My parents would take me home and then go off to a party with the actors, where they analyzed the success of the performance, or God forbid, the lack of it. It was then that I acquired my love for the theater that continues to this day.

Father was also active in the leftist *Poalei Zion-Smol* (Zion Workers-Left) party in town. He was a candidate on behalf of that party at the elections for the Committee of the Jewish Community in 1931. He was second on the list and to his disappointment the party received only one mandate. Ten lists participated in the elections, but the main struggle took place between the Zionist parties and the religious Anti-Zionist *Agudath-Yisrael*.

A group of the Theater activists at the exhibition of paintings of the Director and Artist Ya'akov Rotboim

Sitting from left: P. B. Ravitsky, L. Likhtenshtein, H. D. Shemel, Y. Rotboim, R. Ravitska, Father, and F. Ravitsky

Standing from left: Y. Shtern, M. Khshonstovsky, H. Konfederak, M. Kutshinsky, and Zlotogursky.

The Management Committee for Culture and Drama of the Jewish Theater Society in Wloclawek on the occasion of L. Likhtenshtein's *Aliyah* to *Eretz-Yisrael*, October 1935

First row below from left: H. Konfederak, Y. Shtern and Zlotogursky

Second row from left; F. Ravitsky, M. Pshedetska, L. Likhtenshtein, R. Ravitska and Khshonstovsky

Third row from left: Pshedetsky, D. Pshedetsky, H. A. Tkhuzh, F. B. Ravitsky and Father

Placards of productions in which father was both actor
and director

The Life in Our House

There were five people in our flat at Shpichlerna Street 20: my parents, Grandma, my brother Shemuel and me. The house built of red brick had four floors, street level and three floors. We lived on the second floor along with two other tenants, the Klechevsky family (the owners of the house) and the Levinskys whose daughter Sima was my age and in my class in school. We were very good friends. She was a very beautiful girl with long thick braids. Klechevsky had a daughter Renia and a son Mietek, one year older than me. He belonged to the *Beitar* youth organization and despite the endless arguments between us, suggested that I be his girlfriend. I was 15 years old at the time and I refused, as I did not feel ready for a serious relationship. Anyway, we remained friends.

We had moved to this house in Szpichlerna Street from another house on Krulewiecka Street when I was six years old. The only thing I remember about that house is that it too was made of brick. Our flat was fairly spacious given the conditions of the times in Wloclawek, but a little crowded when compared to today's apartments. The flat consisted of two big rooms, a small one and a kitchen. There was also a small shed on the floor beneath us used mainly to store coal for cooking and heating. During the war it once served as a shelter for Mother and me. Although it was a new house, at first there was no running water. The toilet was in the yard and each tenant had a key for it. The entrance to our house was from the yard, but first through a small one-story house where two Polish families and the concierge lived. In fact, our house stood on a street perpendicular to Shpichlerna, on Browarna Street. Through the window of our flat I could see the Wisla and the tree I described previously. On our visit there in 1994, I found the small bungalow house with the plaster peeling. The municipality had destroyed the house I lived in about 10 years earlier. Only a small section of a wall in Brovarna Street was still there. According to neighbors, who lived across the street, the official reason for razing the house was its instability and danger of collapse. I have doubts about this because the house had been comparatively new.

The Jewish Holidays at Home

My parents were not religious. Our home was kosher, probably due to Grandma and on Friday night she would light candles and Mother prepared the *Shabbath* dinner as usual: gefilte fish, soup, meat etc. Traditional practices were observed on holidays, such as the *Pesakh Seder,* which was held according to custom. We read the whole *Hagadah*, Actually, Father read and we listened not understanding anything. Shemuel and I would ask the Four Questions and also received the answer about The Exodus from Egypt. As children we liked that holiday especially because of the *Afikoman* (piece of matzoth eaten at the conclusion of the Seder). It was exciting to look for it, but it made no difference as to who found it, my brother or me because we both received presents.

On Purim we dressed up in fancy costumes and a festive dinner was arranged at home. We also waited for the *Purim Shpiler*, groups of youngsters in Purim costumes. As a small girl I was a little afraid of them. They would knock on the door, and after opening it we could see strange creatures swaying and singing. Sometimes their singing was more like screaming, but when I grew up I was glad they came. They of course, always received a small coin.

For *Sukkot* a few tenants would build a *Sukkah* in the yard and we would decorate it. About the *Shavuoth* holiday I only remember the tasty dishes Mother prepared, most of them from cheese. The holiday I most enjoyed as a child was *Hanukah*. Snow falling outside, the windows covered with ice flowers, but inside the apartment warm and pleasant with the candles lit. We ate the potato pancakes (*Levivoth*) Mother prepared and later on we played *Dreidl* or cards and lotto with our parents. The atmosphere was relaxed and full of joy and laughter. To this day I feel some warmth and some nostalgia when I recall *Hanukah* at home during my childhood. A week's vacation from school added to the pleasure of this holiday. We went ice-skating or tobogganing almost every day. I, as usual, was a little afraid of sitting on the sled on steep slopes, but summing it up, it was, as the *Sabras*[5] say, *kef* (good fun).

I had ambivalent feelings about *Rosh Hashanah* and *Yom Kippur*. My parents were not religious and did not go to synagogue. Mother was of the opinion that God must be felt in the heart and that it is not obligatory to pray together with others. She believed that prayer on one's own could be even more satisfactory. As a child it was unpleasant when other children asked me where my parents prayed, so I told them that they prayed in the other synagogue. Unlike my parents, Grandma was religious, and in spite of her blindness, she was not ready to give up prayer during the High Holidays. Shemuel and I took her to the synagogue then to her seat in the women's section (*Ezrath Nashim*), after which we went outside into the yard. I did this willingly, because I liked the tumult and the noise the children made when playing, including me. When I grew up this changed, of course. I used to take Grandma to her seat and sometimes I stayed there for a while to feel the atmosphere of that special holiday. I then went home or met up with friends coming back every few hours to check to see if Grandma needed anything. At the end of the day I took her back home.

The Livelihood

As I stated, we were not rich. We had no property, but we lacked nothing at home. Shemuel and I never felt that we lacked anything and we received things we asked for provided they were reasonable. My father owned a small factory for manufacturing cardboard boxes used for packaging shoes, in particular. Three men worked in the plant. They included a somewhat retarded

---

[5] *Sabras* - children born in Israel

Jewish man named Meir whose job it was to clean as well as deliver the boxes to the clients. In addition to Meir there were two Polish workers. One was named Stashek and the other, if I am not mistaken, Vladek. In the morning Father would prepare the work for that day and then go on to other responsibilities. In our town there were four other Jewish families who made their living from the same trade. There was a time when all five, among them the father of Zenek Moshkovitz-Maor, decided to come together to form a big plant. When I came there I was very impressed by the machinery and the many workers. I don't remember when this partnership began and how many years it lasted. The partnership broke up a few years before the war. Everyone took his machinery and workers and established his own business. In our backyard there was a spacious shed that Father rented and where he set up his plant. It looked small compared to the size of the partnership factory.

Shemuel during his Youth

There were just two children in our house: Shemuel (Shmulek) and me, with a small age difference between us. He was born at the end of 1923 and I in the middle of 1922. I heard from my parents that his *Brith* was something special with many people participating. Apparently they were happy with their newborn son. He was a lovely boy with blue eyes and flaxen hair. Mother was very sorry to have to cut his hair and I remember that until the age of five or six he had long hair he rebelled against. He was similar to Mother in looks and to Father in height. The two of us were able to get along well and almost never fought, only once in a while with pillows. I used to be more aggressive, and sometimes if I hit him he would not fight back, but instead remind me that he was also able to retaliate. We were very close and spent much time together. There wasn't any jealousy between us. On the contrary, when Shemuel received a gift when I was not there, he immediately asked: "and for Pola?" I reacted the same way. I think that this loyalty and lack of envy were due to how our parents raised us. They never favored one over the other even when we quarrelled.

When Shemuel was a little boy, and before Grandma lived with us there was a Polish woman who used to take him for a walk. One day she went out with him and did not come back at the usual time. It was getting dark and Mother was almost hysterical. The police were informed. They searched the park, but they were not there. Only when it was completely dark, the woman appeared with Shemuel. As it turned out, she had too much brandy and became tipsy. She then took Shemuel to her flat and fell asleep. Why her house was not searched I'll never understand. I remember this episode more from hearsay than from my own memory, although it seems to me that the details of this event became etched into my mind.

As a child, Shemuel occasionally fainted. I do not know if this was real, but he would suddenly lower his head as though he had fallen asleep. Mother took him to a doctor who recommended that he spend some time in the countryside, out in the woods. So thanks to Shemuel we went to the village of Milenchin every summer for three months. Even after we were at school, we would still go to the village for two and a half months despite the fact that summer school holidays lasted for only two months. At Mother's request, the teachers released us from school two weeks earlier. You can just imagine how envious the other students were. We were good students and in any case during the last two weeks before vacation, nothing new was taught.

Milenchin

The village of Milenchin was four km. (2.5 miles) away from Wloclawek. We went there by narrow gauge railway, by carriage or by horse drawn cart. The peasants' houses were situated on both sides of the yellow soft sand unpaved road and it was possible to walk barefoot without getting injured. The village road was about 1.5 to 2.0 kilometers long, and just a few meters wide.

Behind the houses there were farm buildings and fields. At the ends of the village there were woods. One was called the dry wood because of its dry air. Thanks to its pine trees people with tuberculosis went there. The other was called the humid woods where blackberries and raspberries grew. We picked and ate them with a hearty appetite. There were also mushrooms, called *Kurki*, which we picked, but Mother did not allow us to cook them because she was afraid that some might be poisonous.

Before vacation Mother would rent a house from some peasant, making sure that it would be near the dry woods, which was obviously the main reason for our going there. We would hire a cart with a horse. We would load it with everything we needed in the village including a hammock and a swing, then leave and enjoy the trip. The peasant's house usually had only one room and a kitchen, so he and his family would move into the barn in the yard. There was no electricity in the village and we used a kerosene lamp. As a result, we went to bed early and woke up early. At first, only six Jewish families would stay in the village in summer. Later on the village became so crowded that there was not enough room for everyone, so some of the vacationers went to another village about four kilometres from Milenchin.

In the mornings we would go to the woods with easy chairs, blankets and other necessary items and spend the entire day there except for lunch break. There were many children and youngsters with whom we spent time. We played a lot of volleyball, a game Shemuel and I excelled. Sometimes we were honored and played with the group of the adults when there was a player missing. We also played Croquet, a game Father had bought for us, and of course, hide and seek and other games. We read books (after we had learned to read) and once we even put on a show. There were sand dunes not far away where we would roll down from the top to the bottom, enjoying this immensely. Father joined us every Friday for *Shabbat* and also on Tuesdays, coming by train and bringing goodies and things we could not purchase in the village. The children liked to wait for the train to arrive and welcome all the fathers coming from town. We walked on the rails until the train arrived. One day another boy and I reached the adjacent village by walking on the rails and were almost late for the train. Mother of course, did not know this, and we were lucky to arrive on time, but it required a great effort on our part because we had to run almost all the way back.

Once Shemuel and I were involved in an unpleasant incident while waiting for the train. Shemuel played at throwing stones when he was about eight or nine years old. One stone hit a hut near the rails where Polish men were playing cards. Apparently they were drunk and one upset man, probably the loser in the game, ran out like a wild beast wanting to catch Shemuel who tried to escape. I started to yell so loud that some of the other players came out of the hut, caught the man and held him, so Shemuel was saved. Later on the man apologized.

The trip to the village was always a special experience for me. The fresh air, playing hide and seek among the tall stalks topped with golden ears of corn, the chickens who woke us up in the morning, and the milk Mother brought directly from the cowsheds, all had a charm difficult to describe. A funny thing happened to me, hard to believe that I could have been so naive. There were no stores in the village. Father brought things like sugar, flour, fruits, from town, but we were able to buy milk, butter, cheese and poultry from the peasants. The peasants from the nearby villages brought their products to town once or twice a week, usually walking barefoot with their shoes slung over their shoulders. The road leading to town passed through our village so the vacationing women would go to the peasants to buy needed items. This caused some competition among the women as to who could buy better and cheaper products. For that reason they would wake up earlier and go further up the road to meet the peasants ahead of the others. Mother also took part in this run and we, after waking up would go to catch up with her. One day she asked me to take the butter she had bought home and put it in a cool place while she stayed behind to complete her purchases. I still remember my struggles to find a proper place for the butter. Finally, I decided that the coolest place would be between the cushion and sheet in bed, because every time I put my hand there it felt cool. It was lucky that Mother came home, before the butter melted and soiled the bedding. For many years after that she reminded me with laughter about my "cool place".

A special experience that impressed me very much was the meeting of the *Poalei Zion-Smol* Party in Milenchin where father was one of the activists. I was still a little girl, but I can recall seeing the crowds coming, the joy and the gaiety, and the arrival of Zerubavel, the leader of the party. He was a big man with a long white beard and was the center of attention. I looked at him and was fascinated, as I had never before seen such a beard.

Despite the fact that we enjoyed life in the village very much we preferred to go to the summer and winter camps with our friends from *Hashomer-HaTsair*. We joined the movement when I was 14 after finishing elementary school. In those years Shemuel and I were not only brother and sister, but also good and devoted friends. Shemuel was a good fellow always ready to help and responsible and successful in everything he did. He did not compromise on matters he believed in and could not tolerate hypocrisy, a character trait that did not make his life easy. He was active in the movement and popular in society. After completing elementary school he chose to study in a vocational school. During the war in Russia, in spite of his troubles as a refugee, he managed to learn the locksmith craft especially for shipbuilding. This was his profession in *Eretz-Yisrael*. Additional details about Shemuel's life in the Soviet Union and in *Eretz-Yisrael* are discussed in a later chapter.

Years of Childhood and Learning

When I was born on June 15, 1922 I was named Perl, like all the girls in the family. In fact I was called Pola and my friends call me Pola to this day. This name had a few variations, my Grandma called me Perele, Father by the nickname *Petsush*, and on arrival in *Eretz-Yisrael* my name changed to *Peninah* (pearl in Hebrew). Naturally I do not remember my very early childhood. My first childhood memory, a little obscure indeed, was the story about Shemuel's disappearance with the Polish woman until evening. From a later period I remember the games I played with the children in the backyard of our flat at Krulewiecka Street. Their names have faded from my memory except for the family name Tendler that included two brothers, one my age and the other a little older. I find it odd that I still remember this name, while I have forgotten the names of friends from many years later on. At the age of six we moved to a new flat on Szpichlerna Street. Before reaching compulsory school age that was seven in Poland, I went to a kindergarten, of which I have no memories. I only remember one *Purim* party where I was dressed up as a butterfly, a costume Father made for me.

There were two government elementary schools for Jewish children in town, No. 9 and 10, and the teaching was in Polish. School No.10 was considered the better one, known for its strict discipline. The female principal, an old maid, was highly pedantic and everybody was afraid of her. Students were not allowed to be out on the streets after eight o'clock in the evening or to belong to a youth organization, and woe to the pupil who did not greet the principal in the street with a bow. This applied to all teachers as well. The principal of school No. 9 was a more liberal man, but when it was time for me to go to school my parents chose No. 10. Children attended that school for seven years and upon completion could be accepted at any high school. Our school had no physics or chemistry laboratories; instead we would use those in the Polish school where the children often called us names. Mother indeed warned me about the *Shkotsim* (a nickname for non-Jewish boys), but personally I never encountered any problems from Polish youngsters. Only during their religious holidays when they marched through the streets with pictures of their saints did we not dare to walk on those streets at the same time.

I don't recall any particular experiences from the first day in school, maybe because I was rather fearful at the time. Older children had told me that the teachers would knock you on the knuckles with a ruler and pull your ears if you did not behave properly and this frightened me. I was not used to being hit it as my parents did not use this form of punishment. We would have had to be very naughty indeed to even get smacked on the buttocks.

I still recall how at the age of 11 or 12 Father slapped me in the face and I was so insulted that I did not want to speak to him. It took quite some time, including Mother's intervention before I was able to settle my differences with him. Remarkably, I do not even remember the reason for the slap.

After some time in school my fears evaporated despite the fact that the teachers continued hitting. I attempted to behave and to study hard and do well. In our school all the teachers were women except for one male named Pazhnechevsky. I remember three of the women. One was named Kurtz, young and beautiful and whom we loved very much. Another woman named Shneiberg, was feared by the students. For some reason she liked me perhaps because I was a good student and I liked her history lessons. She managed to portray historical events in such an interesting and vibrant manner that I could see them in my imagination. In the higher grades she was our teacher as well. The third teacher taught crafts and because the children almost drove her crazy I felt very sorry for her. Pazhnechevsky, the only male teacher, taught us Jewish religion. By and large he was a good teacher, but a little too soft so there was not too much discipline in the class. Once I had a small incident with him. He had asked me some question and in his opinion I hadn't answered politely so he requested I apologize. I refused, explaining that I had not said anything offensive. I kept refusing for a long time until teacher Shneiberg explained that she would be forced to reduce my grade in behavior, and so would Mr. Pazhnechevsky. That's when I gave in. In class I was quite popular and was elected to various positions, such as the pupils' committee or the class librarian. The only girl from my class who survived the war was, to the best of my knowledge, Tzelina Leizerowitz, who now lives in Kiryath Hayim. We occasionally did our homework together.

Sometimes I was chosen for small roles in school shows because my father was an actor. I myself did not think that I had any talent for acting. Once, in one of the plays of the *Yiddishe Bine*, a child was needed for a small role of only two sentences. I was chosen, but I failed to say even those two sentences correctly. They then selected Shemuel for that role and he did it well.

The years at school passed smoothly. Only on one occasion was Mother called to the principal because I had gone to *Hashomer-HaTsair* and this was forbidden for pupils of our school. My girl friends had elder brothers who were members of that movement and they invited us to come to their club. We were then 11 to 12 years old and we willingly accepted their invitation. We spent quite some time there until the principal became aware of what was going on and we had to leave. I returned to that movement only after finishing elementary school.

During those years I read many books. At this young age, they were mostly adventure stories like books by Karl May. I knew the names of almost all the Indian heroes by heart, books by Jack London, Jules Verne, Sienkiewicz, Mark Twain, Jane Austin and of course *Little Women* by Louisa May Alcott and later on books by Cronin, Orzeszkowa, Zweig, Hugo and others.

In 1936, at the age of 14, I finished school and the question of what I would do next was discussed. I wanted to continue my studies in high school, but Mother thought that I should also learn a vocation, maintaining that studies without avocation would be useless in Palestine, which was where I wished to go. I think her attitude was influenced by the fact that she herself did not have any vocation. So I applied to the High School of Commerce, but I was not accepted there since it was a Polish high school where only a few Jewish girls studied. Only one girl Jadza

Tsuker from my class was accepted there. Then Mother suggested that I learn needlework in the mornings and continue my studies in a vocational evening school, an idea that did not excite me, but being a good girl, I agreed.

There was a big fashion store in town, which belonged to a Jewish woman named Czeplinska and where many women from the Polish aristocracy had their garments sewn. Mother spoke to the owner and I was accepted as an apprentice. I also paid 300 *zloty* as a tuition fee. I was there until 1:00 PM, then went home, ate lunch and at 3:00 PM went to a Polish government school. The usual subjects were taught including military preparation, similar to a regular high school, but no training in foreign languages or other subjects. Instead we learned accounting. In our class there were two Jewish girls, the daughter of the *Shohet*[6] and I. There was also a Protestant girl who befriended us because the Catholic girls annoyed her. Of course, we did not attend Catholic religion lessons. The relations between the Jewish and the Polish girls were amicable and we had no problems. Incidentally, boys and girls learned in separate, but nearby buildings.

I did not like working in the fashion store so that I did not benefit from this experience. During the year or maybe a little more that I was there, all I managed to learn was how to make a hem and how to complete a garment. I looked for some reason to leave without upsetting Mother. A miracle occurred. I developed eczema on my hands so I left the place and did not come back. After a short time the eczema disappeared and I continued to study in evening school until the war.

In 1936 I joined the *Hashomer-HaTsair* movement. My neighbor Mietek Klechevsky, almost convinced me to join the *Beitar* organization. He was eloquent and his demagogic slogans impressed me at age 14. When I told them at home that I intended to join the *Beitar* organization Father, who was active in the

---

[6] *Shohet* - Slaughterer of chicken, cattle etc. according to the Jewish ritual

leftist *Poalei-Zion* party convinced me that *Beitar* was not a proper organization for me. In addition, my friends Tsela Levin and Esther Jakubovitz followed their brothers and joined *Hashomer-HaTsair* and so did I, a decision I have never regretted. This movement opened up new horizons for me and I can say that in some way it helped me survive the Holocaust.

Hashomer-HaTsair

The *Hashomer-HaTsair* movement in Wloclawek was the biggest and oldest of the Zionist youth organizations in town. It was established in the spring of 1919 by a group of youngsters from the Jewish-Hebrew high school. It began with the help and encouragement of its teachers. It was a magnificent movement consisting of intelligent and idealistic youth. When I joined the movement in 1936 its base was in a two-story building on Kaliska Street that once served as a glassware stockroom. The members of the movement turned it into a beautiful and purposeful club. It was decorated with many ornaments, slogans, pictures from *Eretz-Yisrael* and a big emblem of the movement *Hazak-Ve'ematz* (be strong and of good courage). On the first floor there was a big meeting hall for special occasions, on the second floor a smaller hall for meetings of the *Gedud* [7], as well as six more rooms for meetings of the *Kevutsoth* [8].

There was also a closet with shelves named for each *Gedud*, all members of the organization being divided into *Gedudim*, according to their ages, and every *Gedud* having a Hebrew name: ours being *El-Al*. Every *Gedud* had two instructors, a boy and a girl. Our instructors were Tosia Altman and Kuba (Yakov) Rubin, whom we adored, and they in turn were devoted to us with their heart and soul. To our regret, around 1938 they left us. Tosia

---

[7] *Gedud* - a group of girls and boys of more or less the same age.

[8] *Kevutsa* - a smaller group that included only girls or boys and they together formed the "Gedud."

34

went to Warsaw as a member of *Hanhagah Roshith* the primary leadership of the movement, whereas Kuba went to the States to study. I don't remember the later instructors; apparently their influence on us was minimal. I met Kuba a few times after the war. He lived in *Eretz-Yisrael* for some time and was a lecturer in soil chemistry at the Technion. He was Josef's examiner on this subject when he studied for his Master of Science degree and also visited us later on his trips to *Eretz-Yisrael*.

The activities in the *Gedud* took place once or twice a week and on Saturdays. They included talks and discussions on different themes, ideological lectures or comments on some book that we had to read ahead of time. There were also Hebrew language lessons as well as instruction in songs and folk dances. The *Shabbath* evening parties were fascinating. Whenever we had some time many of us liked to come to the club, as the place was always full of youngsters until late into the night. We would meet with friends from other groups there as well. One of the unforgettable experiences was the *Lag-Ba'omer*[9] excursion. In the early hours of the morning dressed in official uniform, sticks in our hands and bags on our shoulders, we would gather at the club where final arrangements were made. We were organized in rows and went out into the street. A boy with the flag of the movement marched at the head of the group. Behind him drummers beat rhythmically and all of the members of the club marched behind them with enthusiasm and pride. Arriving at the assigned place, usually in the woods near the town, a parade took place and the flag was raised to the top of the flagpole. After singing *Hatikvah* (the anthem of the Zionist Organization and later of the State of Israel) and *Tehezaknah* (the anthem of the socialist wing), the groups dispersed to places marked out for

---

[9] *Lag-Ba'omer* - A holiday between Pesakh and Shavuoth – 33 days after *Pesakh*-when youngsters would go into the woods with arrows and bows in memory of Bar-Kochva's uprising

them. Then sports started; tournaments, learning how to set about camping and, of course, the *kumsitz*[10] around the bonfire with group singing. At sunset, excited and tired, we would return home again marching and singing loudly on Third of May Street where many people on the sidewalks greeted us with applause. They were mostly parents who were happy to see their children return home safely. Among the crowd there were also some Poles and a few made sarcastic remarks as usual, but who cared?

Other experiences I cherished were going to camp during the summer vacation, and the one in winter between Christmas and *Silvester* (New Year's Day), for about one week. The summer camp lasted about two to three weeks and I attended three in 1937, 1938, and 1939. I only attended winter camp once. Here I must again mention Mother with gratitude, that in spite of her anxiety she did not prevent Shemuel and me from participating in those activities. I can imagine that it was not easy for her. As there were neither telephones nor post offices nearby. We would send letters with anyone who went to town. Since there were cases when letters were not given to her Mother, she worried and went to the club to find out what was going on. Once, to my great surprise, she even came to the camp because of a raging storm when thunder and lightning were very frightening, especially where we were in the woods. I don't know how Mother knew about the storm, but she came to see what was going on. The situation was truly bad with the heavy rain having turned the soil into mud that caused the tents to collapse. Our instructors decided that we should return home. In this situation I agreed with Mother coming to camp, especially when more parents also arrived.

By the way, I recall a storm when we were in Milenchin when I was four years old and the wind lifted me up. I actually flew in the air and Mother caught me by my feet. This was my first flight and without a ticket!

---

[10] *kumsitz* - from Yiddish: *kum* - come, *sitz* - sit

Marching at *Lag-Ba'omer*
First line from right: Kuba Rubin, Tosia Altman

The summer camps took place in woods near the small towns of Gombin, Dobrzyn, and Kowel. These were regional camps and they included members from the towns Torn, Poznan, Gdansk, Bydgoszcz, Kutno and some others. Each *Gedud* had a separate place and sometimes also separate activities that were similar to those of *Lag -Ba'omer,* but better organized and diverse. In the morning a parade took place and the flag was raised to the top of the flagpole. We sang the movement anthem *Tehezaknah* and then ate breakfast. After that the day's planned activities began including scouting, sports, outings, meetings and sometimes lectures by someone from town. I think that there were also chores, but I do not remember them exactly. In spite of all the activities there was also free time to enable members from different towns to get to know each other. Among the youngsters from Poznan there were a brother and sister who aroused our interest, both being beautiful youngsters. Their mother was German and their father was Jewish. They had an elder brother who we heard was a member of the *Hitler Jugend*, although they themselves were members of *Hashomer-HaTsair*. It would be interesting to know what happened to them during Nazi rule.

There were rumors that the younger brother tried to reach *Eretz-Yisrael*, but none of my acquaintances know anything of his fate.

During free time I sometimes liked to get away from the tumult, take a blanket and a book and lie down beneath a tree and read without interruption. This was a wonderful period when we were 15-16 years old, youngsters full of energy with a joy of life and romanticism. During this period friendships began between boys and girls, but not like today. These were naive, romantic friendships, which meant going together to the cinema, to the club, taking walks in the park and sometimes maybe sharing a kiss.

A group of girls of *Hashomer-HaTsair*

Bottom line from left: Pola (Peninah) Cypkewicz, Gitla Levi, --, --, Tsesha Rorman

Second line: third from left-Rivkah Tempel

Third line: first from left-Tsela Levin, --, --, Esther Yakubovitz

Above from left: Grinberg (?), Sarah Vishebrotska

On top of the pyramid-Tosia Altman

A *Gedud* (group) of *Hashomer-HaTsair*

From the top: third from left-Blashka, fourth-Hanka Ravitska

Second line: third from left- Hayim Opatovsky, sixth-Pola (Peninah) Cypkewicz

Third line from left: Nathan---, Sarah Vishebrotska, Avraham Goldberg, Rafael Sosnovsky, ---, ---, ---, Fela Levin, Rivkah Tempel

Fourth line from left: Tsesha Rorman, Shlamek Khshontsovsky, ---, Kuba (Ya'akov) Rubin, Tosia Altman, --, Batyah Hulko, Esther Yakubovitz

My First Boyfriend

In the summer camp of 1938 I met a boy from Bydgoszcz (Bidgoshch) named Yisrael (to my regret I forget his family name). He was a nice boy, my age, blond with blue eyes, and spoke Polish with a strong German accent. Bydgoszcz was at one time a German city and many of its inhabitants spoke German as their mother tongue. Yisrael and I became friends and we spent most of our free time together. After camp he returned to Bydgoszcz and I to Wloclawek, but we kept in constant contact by writing letters to one another. In 1939 we met again at summer camp, which lasted, if I am not mistaken, from the end of July until the middle of August. Again we had fun and we were glad to renew relationships with friends. Certainly we could never imagine what awaited us in the very near future. At that camp I met a girl from Bydgoszcz named Janina Gelbert (in the movement she was called Peninah), who stood out from the rest because of her height and her talents in music and poetry. She wrote a poem and Kuba (Ya'akov) Rubin composed music to it. I remember that song until today, rather melancholic words for a young girl, but touching the heart. At the end of camp she invited me to be her guest for a week at her home and it is possible that Yisrael had asked her to do this. After camp I went home, asked for permission to go to Bydgoszcz and about 10-12 days before the war I traveled there. We had no idea that the cursed war was so close. Bydgoszcz is about 100 kilometers (62 miles) northeast of Wloclawek, also on the left bank of the Wisla River, where the river flows straight on northwards to the Baltic Sea. It was a beautiful and very clean city.

I arrived there by train and Janina met me at the station. Arriving at her home, I was surprised at the size and luxury of the flat, something I had never seen before in Wloclawek. It was furnished like a small palace with two entrances; one from the front and one from the kitchen and it had many rooms. I don't recall the exact layout of the flat, but I think that most doors to the rooms led from one to another, like in palaces. I was given a nice room, entirely pink. Janina had an elder sister who was a governess in an aristocratic family. I saw her only once and did not meet the father at all, but their mother was a nice hospitable lady. Every day I would meet Yisrael and we would walk in the town. One evening, sitting on a bench in the boulevard, a policeman approached us and asked Yisrael to identify himself. This astonished me very much since such an action was meaningless to me. Later on I realized that the Poles were afraid of German spies and were therefore suspicious.

After five pleasurable days and enjoyment in Bydgoszcz, Janina came home excitedly and said to me: "Pola, the whole town is a stir, the army is everywhere, people are talking that war will break out soon and it is advisable for you to return home. There could be a situation, where all transportation will be commandeered by the army and then you will not be able to return home." The next day I packed, said good-bye to the Gelberts and to Yisrael, who accompanied me to the train, and traveled home. Arriving in Wloclawek I was surprised to see a calm town and life going on as usual, as if nothing was about to happen. At home I found Mother in the kitchen preparing lunch. This time she was surprised to see me. "Why did you return earlier than planned," she asked, "Did something happen?" I told her what people in Bydgoszcz were saying, that there may be a war soon and that soldiers were everywhere. I had the impression that she and Father, who came home later, did not take my story very seriously. Maybe they did not want to worry Shemuel and me, or maybe they truly believed that it was only talk.

Activities in our club continued and I, having been an instructor for about a year, met with my group who were 12 and 13 years old. Regretfully many years later at the memorial services for Wloclawek Jewry I met only one of them, Erna Blauner and assumed that all the others had died in the Holocaust. Nevertheless, I remember that one or two days before the war tension was also felt in my town. We still hoped that there would be no war that it was only a storm in a teacup, but reality was different. When walking in the street a week or maybe less after I had returned from Bydgoszcz, I heard the voice of the commander of the Polish army Smigly-Rydz saying something like this over the radio: "Citizens, war has broken out, the Germans have invaded our country, but we will fight them. We will not give them even one button from our uniforms, we will show them what Polish soldiers are made of." We wanted so much to believe him. It was Friday, September 1, 1939.

Summary of the Period

Summing up the period of my childhood and youth, I can say that I was rather happy. This does not mean that there were no occasions that made me sad or even caused me to cry, such as being on bad terms with a friend, be it boy or girl, or having expectations that had not been realized. At times reading a book on a bench in the park would help me forget the unease I felt. I was a rather sensitive girl and every injustice according to my understanding bothered me whereupon I would run to Father and ask many questions. I would also be offended if someone made remarks about my imperfect nose, but on growing up I did not pay attention to such remarks since I convinced myself that it did not disturb me, not in school, nor in the movement, in my relations with people or with my suitors. I was an energetic girl (where has that energy disappeared to?) and good at catching balls, running, and jumping. Many times I participated in sport contests when I was in Milenchin. Once during a contest I tried to jump over a fence that was too high for a girl of my age. When I started to run towards the fence somebody shouted, "Hop" spoiling my concentration. The soles of my feet collided with the upper part of the fence, resulting in a somersault in the air and a fall to the ground. My knees were scraped, my hands were scratched, and from then on I no longer jumped over fences. The same thing happened to me when trying to ride a bicycle. I fell off and was injured so I did not try again. Any failure involving injuries or pain discouraged me from trying again.

I was a skinny child, which in those days was not considered nice. Mother would prepare special dishes for me to make me fatter. Since I have no pictures of myself from this period, I will describe myself as follows: a skinny little girl with brown hair, brown eyes, lengthy nose, smooth nice skin, tanned in summer, white straight teeth, dimpled cheeks and a smile which, according to what people said, was charming and inspired sympathy. When I grew up and became a teenager, I did not change much, only became a little fatter. The shape of my face was similar to Mother's, the coloring to Father's. My character too, in spite of my worries, was like Father's. About my dimples, when I met Shemuel in *Eretz-Yisrael* after years of not seeing each other he reminded me how Mother had explained to him how the dimples were created. She would put two peas on my cheeks and bind them with a handkerchief for the night. I was greatly moved that he remembered this funny story, as I didn't.

So far I have described the quiet and orderly life at home, which changed abruptly in 1938, when Mother became ill. One day she began to suffer from a strong headache and the pills she took helped her for only a few hours. At first the doctors could find no reason for these pains. The many pills she took made her a little dizzy, so she shut herself up and stayed in bed a lot. Suddenly, the atmosphere in our house became different, although we managed more or less. A Polish girl would come once a week to clean the flat and an elderly woman who saw to our laundry, as well as Grandma who, despite her blindness, would help Mother. She would even sew, and people did not believe that she was really unable to see. At this time I stayed at home during the morning hours. In fact, I was supposed to study advanced accounting in Popiolek's private school in order to complete my studies, but Mother's illness caused me to leave after a short while. It was sad to be at home and to see Mother suffering without being able to help her. Only after a few weeks did the doctor come to the conclusion that the headache was caused by high blood pressure, and he decided to put leeches on her neck behind her ears, to suck her blood. These were black worms, four cm in length, which thrive on blood. This was the customary method to reduce blood pressure. It helped Mother for some time until the pains returned and then it was necessary to repeat the treatment with the leeches. This situation lasted for a long time, maybe a year, until the pains stopped and life at home returned to normal. The death of Grandma on *Pesakh* 1939 at the age of 83 was painful, but we were grown up enough to understand that life does not last forever. We were left with pleasant memories of her and that is certainly satisfying.

At War

On that bitter day, September 1, 1939, the war began. I was on the street when this became apparent to me and I quickly ran home. I was scared, because I had heard from German Jewish refugees who had managed to escape what the Nazis were doing to the Jews who lived there. Father tried to calm us by relying on the radio propaganda; namely that the Polish army was powerful and there was a chance that the Germans would not reach Wloclawek at all. If this happened, it would not be as bad as one had heard. He knew the Germans from World War I, and thought it possible to get along with them. By the third day of war the Polish army began to disintegrate and the Germans rapidly advanced into Poland. There was panic and people began to escape. We hired a cart like so many others, loaded it with some of our belongings and began to trek eastwards in the direction of the Russian border. The roads were crowded with many vehicles as well as many people who walked on foot, while German *Stuka* airplanes flew over the heads of the refugees and shot at them. Each time we saw planes approaching, we ran to the ditches beside the road and lay down in them. It was very frightening to us, but for the German pilots it was surely fun to shoot at unarmed men, women and children. We did not get very far and to our dismay bumped into the German Army entering a village on our way. I remember the scene as if it happened today. We stood on the sidewalk and the German soldiers according to the famous German *Ordnung* marched by. My parents decided to return home probably because they realized the roads were blocked and it was senseless to continue. So after an absence of two or three days we came back to Wloclawek. At night we slept in the ditches beside the road.

Under Nazi Rule

The German Army entered Wloclawek on September 14, 1939; two weeks after the war began. Units from the SS and the Gestapo entered the city together with the Army and immediately issued different edicts against the Jews. Father still believed that the devil was not so terrible that they don't kill people without any reason. It so happened that one German came to us and ordered a few cardboard boxes and even paid for them. Very soon it became clear; the devil was not only bad, but also unbelievably cruel.

S.A. Sturmbannfuerer Hans Kramer was appointed mayor of the town and Eliot Hasamayer was appointed his deputy; Hasamayer was hanged in Wloclawek after the war. Most sickening of all was that their advisor on Jewish affairs was a German named Max Dunkhorst, a resident of the town. For many years before the war he was the gymnastics teacher in *Maccabi* and in the Hebrew high school and was friendly with his fellow teachers. These three men were the main officials responsible for all the *Actions* that deprived the Jewish population of their possessions. The abuses and horrors started on September 24th with the burning down of the two synagogues, the old one on Zabia Street and the new one on Krulewiecka Street. The climax of outrageousness was that about ten Jews who lived near the synagogues were accused of setting that fire and were arrested.

The first victims fell during the night of *Kol-Nidrei* (*Yom Kippur eve*). In a house on Lengska Street not far from the street where we lived people had gathered for prayer. On their way home a patrol of SS men noticed them and started shooting. The victims both living and dead were buried together in the backyard of the house where the prayers had taken place. The pit was excavated by neighborhood Jews taken from their homes for that purpose. Later those murdered were reburied in the Jewish cemetery. We received the news about this incident almost immediately and it was difficult for me to believe that people were able to commit such horrors. Tension and fear dominated everyone at home and in town. At night we hardly slept as every move and every noise frightened us.

One afternoon when Mother and Shemuel were not at home Father and I suddenly heard heavy footsteps on the stairs of the house and the shouting of *Juden raus*! (Jews, get out!) After that, shouting and crying from the floor above us people were running downstairs. I opened the door and two armed Germans stood in front of me. One of them looked quite normal, but the other looked like a wild beast and he shouted at the people *schneller, schneller* (faster, faster) and also hit them. When Father came out onto the staircase, I begged the German, who looked more human, to leave Father alone. The other one was upstairs checking that no one was left. He shouted at me "be quiet," pushed me against the wall put his revolver to my head and ordered Father to go down the stairs. To this day I ask myself how it happened that I was not scared, but only wondered if he would shoot or not, as if it was not really a question of life or death. I also do not understand why he stood beside me with his revolver pushed against my head until his colleague went downstairs. Then he left me and went down too. He could have pulled the trigger, he could have thrown me down the stairs because I was disrupting from him doing his job, but he stood there as though he was trying to protect me from the other one, which was hard to believe. After some time Mother returned home. She already knew that Father had been taken away, but we did not know what happened to Shemuel. We were very worried and hardly survived the night, but in the morning Shemuel came home. He had been in a friend's house and on hearing what was going on had hidden and had not been found.

The detained men were taken to the municipal jail and after a few days transferred to the barracks of the 14th battalion which does not exist anymore. From there they were taken to do menial work. The following day we found out where Father was working and I went to see him. I was surprised that the guards allowed me to approach and talk to him. Father asked me to bring him food, which I did for the next two days until the Germans did not allow anyone near the place anymore. One day a man was shot when marching in line under escort because his wife tried to pass him some food. A woman was drowned in the Wisla because she went outside before the curfew ended. After 10 or 14 days the group was freed and among them Father, but not before the Jewish community had been ordered to pay the municipality 100,000 *zloty.* After a short time we had to pay 200,000 more and after another week an additional 250,000.

When father returned home we were thrilled and excited, but that did not last for long. On the same day in the afternoon Shemuel was detained. This was a very painful surprise. We had thought he was more or less safe because he was working for the Germans somewhere, but we were mistaken. In order to relax a little from what happened to Father I went out in the afternoon to meet some friends. On my way I saw a group of Jews in the street all with their hands up, led by German soldiers. Suddenly, as if lightening had struck me, I saw Shemuel among them. I still remember the shock I felt, the helplessness, the anger and the hate for those pretending to be human beings. I ran home and said crying: "Mother, they took Shemuel." I didn't tell her about the raised hands because I knew that this would upset her terribly. We began to search to find out where he was. It turned out that the group had been taken to jail. I don't remember if they were taken to work or not. Fear was pervasive and people, mostly youngsters started to leave Wloclawek for other towns where the situation was not so bad yet. Others escaped eastwards into the part of Poland that had been occupied by the Russians. Our neighbor's son Mietek also escaped, but I don't know where he went or what happened to him.

After about 10 days of worry the Germans freed all on condition that the community supply 800 men for work every day. When Shemuel returned home the family met and jointly decided that he and Father would go eastwards to Lomza a town under Russian rule where father had a cousin. I suggested that we all go, but Mother objected, saying that it was not reasonable to abandon everything and just leave. There was no mention as yet in those days that women could possibly be abused. Mother thought that after Father and Shemuel arrived in Lomza they would write to us and then we would join them. Oh, how naive we were!

For the next two days Father and Shemuel did not leave the house to lessen the danger of being abducted by the Germans. Meanwhile Mother prepared the necessary things for the trip and on the designated day Mother and I went to see them off. The parting was painful. The picture of how they looked through the window of the train as they waved goodbye is etched deeply into my heart. I couldn't imagine then that I would never see Father again. We came back home hoping that soon we would all be together again, but fate turned out differently.

Meanwhile, the situation in Wloclawek worsened. More and more edicts were issued against the Jews. It was forbidden for Jews to walk on the sidewalks, only in the road; Jews had to take their hats off for every uniformed German; Jews had to wear a yellow triangular patch on their back to humiliate them. Wloclawek was the first town in Poland where the yellow patch was introduced on the October 25, 1939. The Jews in town were exposed to cruel terror and persistent fear. The Germans would enter their houses and rob whatever they could lay their hands on. Life became unbearably hard. In addition, the deportations started. On the December 1, 1939 thousands of Jewish families were deported to Ozerov (a town in Poland), including my Uncle Alter his wife and their young daughter.

Due to the terror and the tense atmosphere that permeated the town Mother decided we should leave Wloclawek and join her sister Malka in Warsaw until the danger passed. Who could have ever thought or expected what was to happen afterwards? We packed a few things, locked the door and traveled to Warsaw by train. This was at the beginning of December 1939, and at this time there were no ghettos in Poland yet. Jews were still allowed to travel freely from one place to another. From Wloclawek it was possible for us to travel in freight wagons only. It was an uncomfortable and unforgettable journey.

We traveled in an open wagon and it was very cold, the winter of 1939-40 being particularly hard with the temperature dropping to minus 25°C (-12F°). We sat wrapped up in a corner of the wagon huddled together, hoping that by sitting this way we would be warmer. The train stopped very often and we were afraid that German soldiers would throw us out or rob us. The trip that normally took two hours, lasted many, many, tension filled hours. We were really frozen, but felt relief when we finally arrived in Warsaw at my aunt's and her family's house. She immediately prepared hot tea and a meal for us.

Chapter 2: Warsaw
Life in the Occupied City

My first impression of Warsaw as compared to Wloclawek was as if we were living in paradise. People walked on the sidewalks not in the road and Jews were not wearing a yellow patch on their backs. Actually, from December 1st all Jews were required to wear a white stripe on the right arm 10 cm wide with a *Magen-David* on it, but this looked less humiliating than the yellow patch. I also did not feel the tension and the fear in Warsaw that dominated Wloclawek. I learned quickly that the situation here was not at all like my first impressions. There were different edicts here yet life seemed to be more bearable.

We stayed with my aunt, but paid for our food. Mother had some jewels and whenever necessary she sold some. In addition, the refugees from Wloclawek established a soup kitchen with the help of the *Joint* (American Jewish Joint Distribution Committee) an international organization for helping Jewish people all over the world. It was there that Mother was able to get a job. At this time my aunt's economic situation was still satisfactory since she still worked in the family candy factory.

My first unpleasant encounter with the Germans in Warsaw happened a few days after our arrival. One day I was walking in the street with Shlamek Khshonstovsky, a member of our movement. Suddenly there was a raid by German soldiers taking people from the streets, probably for work. There was uproar and people began to run in different directions. We also began to run, the crowd separating us. I returned home, but I don't know what happened to Shlamek. Probably he was caught and sent to some work camp. People said that the work in itself was not the worst part, but rather the mistreatment. The manhunt frightened the Jewish population and many did not dare to leave their homes.

In January 1940, about two months after arriving in Warsaw, ration cards were introduced. The card owner had to be registered in a licensed food store. At first the Jews received the same cards as the Poles, but very soon were given cards of another color and their ration of food was reduced. I remember that to obtain the ration card one had to get an injection (maybe because of the typhus that raged in the city). I had never received any injection before and I was very frightened. At first I refused to submit, but later on I gave in.

What could I do? Did I have a choice? (How foolish it was for me to make an issue of this). Warsaw was flooded with refugees who had managed to escape from the areas that had been annexed to the Third Reich. In those areas there raged unbelievable terror. Most of the refugees left their homes with few if any possessions and thus needed aid. The Germans also expelled the Jews from smaller communities and brought them almost breadless to Warsaw. They lived in special places for refugees or with relatives. It was very crowded everywhere, but the worst thing was that there was no work. *(In 1939 there were 380,000 Jews in Warsaw. In 1940 the number increased to 393,000 and in March 1941 it further increased to 445,000).*

The Germans had cut off most of the Jews' sources of making a living except for the food stores that operated under license. People were hungry and didn't have the money to buy food that was still available at very high prices. The *Joint* helped by establishing a public soup kitchen where everybody could get a dish of watery soup once a day. The hunger, the cold and the crowding caused illnesses mainly typhoid fever. *(From September 1939 until August 1942, 88,570 people died in the ghetto, of them 76,000 from hunger and diseases)* In order to fight this the city officials locked houses, disinfecting the flats and sending the tenants to a public bathhouse. One day our house was also locked for disinfecting and we were sent to a bathhouse. There our clothes were taken for disinfecting and it was not difficult to guess what they looked like afterwards. A Jewish woman decided to make a living from this situation and caused the most humiliating event in this process. She would take advantage of her job as the so-called "supervisor" of women's cleanliness. She issued a ruling directed mainly to young women whose appearance was still acceptable stating that their hair was dirty and heads would have to be shaved. After being paid a sum of money she would cancel her ruling. When she did the same to me I was very insulted and scared. I cried, asking her to leave me alone, but she was not impressed. Only the 5 *zloty* Mother gave her allowed my hair to suddenly be clean.

Two or three months after arriving in Warsaw my uncle Mintz took me to the small town of Wolomin where he lived with his family. This town was about 20 kilometers (16 miles) from Warsaw and the railway from there to Grodno passed through it. When I arrived there life was the same as before with Jews and Poles living together. The time I spent there I didn't see any Germans. (This was at the beginning of 1940. What happened later I don't know).

My uncle who didn't look Jewish traveled to Warsaw every day. What type of business he had I don't remember or maybe I never knew, but I assume that he traded with the Poles. He and his wife had four daughters and a younger son. Two of the girls were about my age so I had people to spend time with. Sometimes friends would come to visit including a Polish young man who came from time to time and courted their eldest daughter Bronka.

Renewed Contact with the Movement.

While I was staying with my uncle my instructor in *Hashomer-HaTsair* in Wloclawek, Tosia Altman, met Mother and told her that a so-called "kibbutz" from the movement in Warsaw was to be organized. She recommended I join it. Here I must write a few words about the leaders of the movement. At the beginning of the German invasion many members of the leadership, and in fact from the whole movement, escaped to Vilna (Vilnius) that was then the capital of Lithuania. They thought that from there they could go to *Eretz-Yisrael*, but very few succeeded. Meanwhile it became clear to these members in Vilna that the youth in Poland were helpless and that there was hunger among them and nobody to lead them. According to the movement's decision a few members of the leadership returned to Nazi occupied Warsaw in order to organize them anew. Among them were: Mordehai Anilevitz, later to be the commander of the Warsaw Ghetto uprising; Joseph Kaplan, senior activist in the underground; Tosia Altman, a fighter in the uprising; Shemuel Braslav, who was responsible for the underground newspaper; and Aryeh Vilner, one of the leaders of the underground. I am full of praise and admiration for those young adults, the eldest among them being Josef Kaplan, 27 years old and the others in their early twenties. They left what was a safe place in those days and returned to the Nazi inferno. They immediately started to organize the movement, to look for jobs and to provide help for its members. Between February and April 1940 Tosia concentrated on searching for members who had dispersed during the war. This activity necessitated visits to towns and cities in Poland and these travels exposed her to many dangers in spite of her non-Jewish looks. Wherever she arrived, happiness was indescribable. It must be remembered that the Jews at that time were disconnected from the world, even from other towns in Poland. Tosia's appearance was like a beam of light connecting them to the world and in fact, sometimes even to their parents. She would deliver information, encourage and also bring money for organizing the youth. The money came from the *Joint* and from the movement abroad, if I am not mistaken. Later she would maintain contact between the ghettos that were tightly closed. She would enter the ghettos with an outside working group and in the same way leave them. It was very dangerous. She traveled as a Polish girl and had to always be on guard so that she would not to be caught.

Kibbutz Ma'apilim

Thanks to the leadership's efforts a town kibbutz was established in Warsaw named *Ma'apilim*. There young people from Krakow and Wloclawek who were living as refugees in the city joined the young adults from Warsaw. Thanks to Tosia I was also among them. Looking back, I think that in some way the kibbutz helped me to survive.

After Mother met Tosia who told her about the kibbutz, Mother delivered that message to me through my uncle and I immediately decided to join it. There was only one problem. In those days it was already forbidden for Jews to travel by train and my looks were not very Aryan. When I first went to stay with my uncle this order did not exist. Nevertheless, I decided to risk it since I had enough of staying with uncle's family. Although they treated me well I felt that it was time for me to leave. I also wanted to see Mother and to be with my friends so I decided to go back to Warsaw. My uncle traveled on this line every day and agreed to travel with me in the same train, even in the same carriage, but not together only as strangers, in order not to endanger him with my Jewish looks. He gave me some useful advice such as to mix with elderly people, to sit near a window, to look outside, etc. The next day I dressed nicely with my light summer coat and a beret, hiding the white stripe with the *Magen-David* on my sleeve, with a scarf. If I would be caught without the stripe at best I would be taken to the police station or to jail or at the very worst, shot. The trip passed successfully. Now I had to exit the station through a gate where two policemen stood checking tickets as well as the people. Here the advice from uncle had been to mingle into the middle of the crowd and to push together with them through the gate, which is what I did and fortunately it worked. I arrived at my Mother's (there was as yet no ghetto in Warsaw) and after a few days I joined the kibbutz. I think it was May or June 1940.

Tosia Altman

The flat of the kibbutz at Nalevky Street No 23 was spacious enough. I don't remember exactly, but according to my friend Rachel Beker's description there was a kitchen, quite a large dining room, and two bedrooms, one for boys and the other for girls. There was also another small hidden room where the activists met and which housed the typewriter and the mimeograph for printing the underground newspaper. On the floor above the kibbutz there was a public kitchen from the *Joint* and another big hall in which lectures were delivered from time to time.

Despite the bad economic conditions there was intense activity in the kibbutz, even debates on ideological issues. There was also a library that became a meeting point for members of the movement in Warsaw. It should be pointed out that in the years of 1940 to 1941 no one had any inkling about the Nazis' satanic plans and extermination camps. It was generally thought that there could be more decrees, maybe even some pogroms and killings of individuals, but the systematic murder of an entire nation seemed impossible and did not enter anyone's mind. The idea seemed so terrible that no one could envision that even beasts like the Nazis could execute such a plan.

In August 1940 the city was divided into three sections: German, Polish and the Jewish ghetto. In the middle of November of that year the ghetto was sealed with a high brick wall three meters high and 18 kilometers long (10 feet by 11 miles). The construction was financed by the ghetto Jews.

The economic situation of the Jews in the ghetto became worse with each passing day. The Germans supplied a small quantity of commodities for the ration cards, but the main source of commodities were the smugglers. Cars or trucks coming through the gate with the help of the three police forces who guarded the gate carried out most of the smuggling. The guards were the Germans, the Poles and the Jews. Clearly, all of them received much money for it, especially the Germans. People who worked outside the ghetto conducted small-scale smuggling through holes in the wall. All smuggling was very dangerous and punishable by death. Therefore prices soared and only the rich could eat to satisfaction. Others sold everything possible, everything that the Germans had not yet stolen: gadgets, jewelry, clothes and anything that could be exchanged for a piece of bread. Those people who had nothing to sell could not survive on the one plate of daily soup supplied by the *Joint*, and many died from cold, hunger and illnesses. In the streets you could see many corpses covered with paper. It was a shocking sight, but the ghetto inhabitants, hungry themselves and not knowing what the morrow would bring, were almost indifferent. Even I, always sensitive to human suffering became desensitized to the sight after the initial shock. I was able to pass by the corpses without much emotion since there was nothing I could do about them.

Despite this situation and the constant German terror there was cultural activity in the ghetto. There were theaters performing shows, skits and satires. Only once I was able to attend a performance in a theater thanks to a free ticket I received. There also were schools and apparently an orchestra.

In the kibbutz the situation was not easy since food was scarce and we were always hungry. The daily menu was more or less very limited. In the morning we had two slices of bread with some spread and a drink. I don't recall what lunch was except most likely soup with one slice of bread. In the evening we had two slices of bread and some drink. The comrades working outside (mainly the men) received one or two sandwiches. The money for maintaining the kibbutz came from the work of its members, the *Joint* and parcels from abroad, mainly from Switzerland. In those days the mail still functioned for Jews too. These parcels included very valuable items needed in the ghetto that were exchanged for money. The boys worked hard in the German factories and sometimes also had temporary jobs where the danger of being sent to a labor camp was great. The girls were busy primarily doing domestic work in the kitchen, cleaning, laundry and the like, but there were some who also worked outside as housekeepers or nannies. I worked for a few days in a comb factory. This was very unpleasant work and I remember that I stood in water all day. One day I also worked as a lady's helper (there were people who still had money). Apparently I was not satisfactory because the hosts didn't want me to return. I was not used to doing cleaning work, much less doing it quickly. Finally I would take turns of duty at the kibbutz where a good place to work was in the kitchen, enabling you to get another slice of bread or a little more soup. A Warsaw girl named Tamara who was very nice and a well-liked member of the kibbutz was in charge of the kitchen.

One day Tosia asked me if I would like to learn in a school and since I was glad to have the opportunity, I agreed. What exactly we learned there I don't remember anymore except for mathematics and zoology. Why zoology? I don't know. Maybe there was a teacher for this subject. I remember the mathematics lessons well because of the teacher. When he entered the class for the first time I was shocked by his looks. He looked like some caricature with a hunchback, but when he started to speak, to explain, he became so interesting a person that I forgot about his poor looks. I recall his lessons to this day, but I have to point out that the curriculum was not like in normal times, but was adjusted to the reality of the time.

One day I heard from Rachel Beker that Yisrael, my friend from Bydgoszcz, had been looking for me and promised to come to the kibbutz the next day. I had a dilemma since I didn't want to continue the friendship and I was not in a frame of mind for any commitment at that time. On the other hand I did not have the courage to tell him so I chose the easiest way out. I simply didn't appear the next day. Even now I haven't forgiven myself for this childish behavior. In 1940 we didn't realize a terrible Holocaust would come later and that we would not see each other again and I would never be able to explain. Nevertheless, it still disturbs me when I recall it.

The wooden bridge connecting two sides of the walled Warsaw ghetto that was divided by a street with a tramway in its center.

In the kibbutz at Nalevky No 23, life was active in spite of the hunger, the hard work and the German abuse. Every time Germans were seen in the ghetto fear became apparent. But we were all young and we still believed in a better future. Among the members of the kibbutz those living in Warsaw were helped by their parents. From time to time they would go home to eat something (provided that the parents still had some food) and sometimes even brought something to their friends. Mother worked in the kitchen of the Wloclawek refugees and almost every day would bring me some food at my aunt's. It was not quite legal, but the manager of the kitchen, Mr. Tsigansky, one of the former heads of the Jewish community in Wloclawek, was a very nice and understanding man and gave his quiet approval, especially since he knew Father. After a few months Mr. Tsigansky left the kitchen for reasons unknown to me. A woman named Shmietanska, a former Latin teacher in the Jewish High School in town and a civilized, but bad person replaced him. When she became aware that Mother was taking some food outside, she fired her. Mother's explanation that it was only something small for her daughter didn't help. This was a big blow for us, mainly for Mother who by now was left almost without any means.

At first Mother didn't tell me about her dismissal because she didn't want to worry me. She was always a very loving and devoted mother and always wanted to save us from any unpleasantness.

So Mother remained without work and I felt guilty because this had happened because of me. She still had a few things to sell, but people took advantage of other people's sufferings and would only pay pennies. I didn't want her to give things away for nothing, so I decided to forego my lunch at the kibbutz and to take it to her. I didn't want the kibbutz members to know about it, so that when the meal was being handed out I would put it aside saying that I would eat it later. After everyone had gone I would take the slice of bread and the soup and bring it to Mother. Actually it took a great deal of strength not to give in to my hunger. Only people who have suffered hunger can understand that effort, but I owed it to Mother. I also had a problem not only concealing from her that this was my meal, but to persuade her that it was her meal, otherwise she might have refused altogether. This arrangement lasted for two or three weeks. One day she told me that she had received a letter from Uncle Alter in Ozerow in which he wrote that they are managing quite well and that he was inviting her to come to them and that she was willing to accept the invitation. I suspect that she realized somehow that I was lying to her about her meal and that she wanted to make my life easier because her first concern was for us, her children. After the war I learned from Uncle Alter who had survived, that Mother was the one who had appealed to him for help and that he had then suggested that she join him and his family.

It turned out that Tamar, the kitchen manager also suspected that I was not eating my lunch, but seeing that I was hiding it didn't say a word. When she saw me eating my lunch again she broached the subject and when I told her the truth, she was angry with me, because I hadn't asked her for help. Apparently my pride had held me back. By the way, I heard later that the Wloclawek kitchen was closed anyway after a short while.

One or two months before the ghetto was closed Mother left Warsaw (the exact date I don't remember). We separated, believing that it was only for a short time. Who could have imagined that we would never meet again? I received two postcards from her. In the first she informed me that she had arrived safely at my uncle's, but it didn't mention how she had traveled. The second one was an answer to my letter in which I told her that there was a possibility of going to *Eretz-Yisrael* and that I intended to sign on. She implored me not to do so because she had heard that all those who registered were murdered. She wrote this in camouflaged form and later it became clear that all the talk about *Aliyah* was mere lies. After that second postcard, contact between us was cut off. Meanwhile, in November 1940 the ghetto was closed, and the situation in Warsaw became more and more acute. During 1942 43,000 people died in the ghetto from hunger and disease.

In the kibbutz, life didn't change very much, but it became more difficult for the *Shelihim-Kasharim* (members of the movement and mostly young women with non-Jewish features and with Polish documents able to travel from place to place). They maintained the connection between the underground and us and from the other ghettos. They brought information as to what was happening in the so-called "work camps" that in most cases were really death camps.   One day Tosia appeared and told us a terrible story that made our hair stand up on end. The Germans were transporting Jews in sealed trucks and poisoning them to death using the exhaust gases of the engines. I was shocked, and found it very difficult to believe this story. I left the meeting and walked the streets without being able to calm down and seeing poisoned people in my mind, all the time asking myself: "Why? What had we ever done to these damn Germans?"

Chapter 3: Zharky

The Farm in Zharky

This farm was near the small town of Zharky, about 25 kilometers (16 miles) southeast of the big town of Czestochowa. It was a neglected farm, owned by a Jew, which had been expropriated and given by the authorities to a German firm. After great efforts Tsevi Brandes from Zharky, an active member of *Hashomer-HaTsair*, succeeded in obtaining a permit to cultivate the land. The movement leaders in Warsaw, particularly Tosia Altman and Josef Kaplan also made great efforts to get back the farm in Czestochowa, which before the war was a training place (*Hakhsharah*) for members of the movement before their *Aliyah* to *Eretz-Yisrael*. Unfortunately they weren't successful in having their wish fulfilled. The leadership tried to take as many young members of the movement as possible out of Warsaw, with the aim of improving their lives, and making room in the kibbutz at Nalevky Street for other members. The care displayed by the leadership for the young members deserves praise and admiration. In the spring of 1941 Tsevi Brandes, Josef Kaplan and perhaps Tosia began to transfer the members of Kibbutz *Ma'apilim* in Warsaw to Zharky. This operation was not simple, because Jews were forbidden to be outside the ghetto or to travel by train. To leave the closed ghetto that was encircled by a high wall was also dangerous. Some of the members, who didn't look typically Jewish, left through the gate of the ghetto together with some work groups, and when outside they would leave the group carefully so as not to be seen by the patrols. There was always a threat that Poles would identify them and hand them over to the Germans. Rachel Beker (later-Tratsevitzky), for example, went out as a Polish girl together with Tosia. I don't really know how others with non-Aryan appearances managed to leave the ghetto. I imagine that the majority went out like me, through a hole in the ghetto wall, with Josef Kaplan as a guide. He had a permit enabling him and one companion to travel by train, but this permit was not valid outside the ghetto. It seemed illogical, but who expected the Germans to be logical.

I left the ghetto in the summer of 1941. Josef Kaplan and I left through a hole in the wall at Shjena Street, which according to Aryeh Gutkind, a member of the kibbutz, was the closest place to the railway station. Smugglers had made these holes to bring food into the ghetto. Outside the ghetto, we put our coats over our arms to hide the stripe with the *Magen-David* on it. Although we both looked Jewish, Josef Kaplan in particular, the Germans really could not identify Jews as such; the problem was the Polish informers. We hadn't gone far from the wall, when a Polish boy, about 13 to 14 years old, came up and said: "Jews, you are Jews." I must admit, that I was very scared and my heart was beating rapidly, as I already could see us in Gestapo hands. Josef Kaplan calmed me down: "Don't be afraid, he only wants some money." There were opportunistic Poles who would hide near the wall and upon seeing someone leave through these holes, would follow them and ask for money. It seems that Josef Kaplan had experienced this situation, so he gave 5 *zloty* to the youngster who then disappeared, and we continued on our way to the railway station. I can't say how long it took to reach the station, but to me it seemed like an eternity. Every person we met, Polish or German, caused my heart to beat rapidly. Fortunately we arrived safely at the station, where our presence was legal. To minimize the danger of identification, these trips would be carried out during late afternoon hours when it was safer. The train brought us to a small station near Czestochowa and from there a member of the kibbutz took us by coach to the farm in Zharky.

Being on the farm was like being on another planet. The place was quiet and beautiful and best of all, there were no Germans. It was paradise. The yellow cornfields, fruit trees, and the garden with its growing vegetables along with my feelings of freedom made me indescribably happy and excited. My friend Lilka and I ran joyfully in the fields among the tall corn stalks, deeply breathing the fresh air. It was like a dream and so different from the Warsaw Ghetto, that for a while we forgot all the misery that Hitler had brought on us as Jews.

I don't remember much about the living conditions on the farm, nor the house we lived in or the food we ate, but I do remember working in the garden. I liked the work very much in spite of my hands being uncomfortably cold in the autumn when I was harvesting potatoes. This isolated farm also served as a shelter and a hiding place if needed, as well as a meeting place for the leadership and the *Kasharim* (youth who maintained connections with the underground). At the end of the agricultural season, regretfully most of us had to leave because of unemployment. Only four people remained for some time afterward to guard the farm. We moved to Czestochowa, where we established a kibbutz at Berek Joselewitz Street No 1. A coach harnessed to a horse carried out the move for us.

Chapter 4: Czestochowa
Life in the Ghetto

Czestochowa (pronounced: Chenstochova) was an industrial town about 200 kilometers (125 miles) southwest of the capital city of Warsaw (Warszawa). It is famous for the Church of *Jasna Gora* in which there is an old picture of "The Black Madonna." According to Christian belief, she affected miracles and even nowadays tens of thousands of pilgrims from all over Poland come to see her. In 1939 before the war, about 28,000 Jews lived in Czestochowa, about 20% of the total population. The Jews made a living from commerce, industry and crafts.

When I arrived in Czestochowa at the end of 1941 after my few happy and quiet months in Zharky, a Jewish ghetto was already in the city. It had been set up on April 9, 1941. A Jewish Committee (*Judenrat*) was functioning in the ghetto. They established most of the institutions for making life in this terrible situation bearable, like the Jewish Police, and the medical, work, and education bureaus. The Germans issued an order that every Jew should wear a white stripe with a blue *Magen David* on the left arm. Jews were forbidden to travel by train. Jewish factories and shops were transferred to Germans (*Treuhaendler*) and many of the Jews were taken to forced labor in different locations of Poland.

The ghetto was not fenced because it was situated in the middle of the city. Poles could cross from one side to the other, but Jews were forbidden to leave the ghetto under threat of death. When Poles crossed through the ghetto, they were forbidden to stop or to enter a shop or a house. The Germans pretended that this edict was necessary because of infectious diseases in the ghetto. In spite of notices to this effect, the Poles would stop; even do business with the Jews making it possible to buy food from the Poles for money, for clothes or for other items. The particular site of this ghetto eased the lives of the Jews and so the situation was incomparably better than in the Warsaw Ghetto.

Indeed hunger and poverty existed here as well due to the German orders as in all the other cities. Here people were snatched for forced labor and there were murders, but on the whole the atmosphere was different and quieter. People still believed that most of the Jewish population would not be harmed. It was a unique ghetto, populated by 50,000 to 60,000 Jews. It included the Jews from Czestochowa and its surroundings, as well as those Jews who the Germans had banished from small villages and people who had come on their own initiative, believing that it was still possible to live here.

At the Kibbutz in Czestochowa

Arriving in Czestochowa, I also had the impression that the situation was not so bad here, that here people were calmer and the streets were nice and clean. At the kibbutz in Joselewitz Street we were 12 to14 members. The flat in which we lived was a restored shed, with partitions to make three rooms, a bedroom for the boys, and a bedroom for the girls, and a combined dining room and kitchen. The conditions were hard. There was no running water in the flat. We had to bring water in from the backyard. Typically, we would wash ourselves from a pail, but occasionally we went to the public bathhouse. I don't remember where the lavatory was, probably in the courtyard.

The boys worked hard at the *Ostbahn*, changing railway sleepers. Aryeh Gutkind recalled that they would rise at 4:30 AM to catch the 5:00 AM train to Rudniky, where they worked until dark. After work they were forced to wait in the cold for a few hours for the train that would bring them back to Czestochowa. They returned to the kibbutz, cold and uncomfortable, late in the evening causing friction with our instructor Miriam Heinsdorf, from Warsaw. They argued that she made no attempts to arrange easier work for them, and finally she was sent away. The girls had an easier life, most of the time we worked in the home. For a period I worked in a factory outside the ghetto, where I sewed aprons from some kind of paper. It is here that I met Uta Vargon, who later became Stefan Grayek's[11] wife. This was work without pressure and more importantly, without German supervisors. I also worked outside the ghetto weeding the garden and yards of a German school with a group of 20 girls including my friend Lilka. In the morning we would get the tools from an elderly Polish man who was in charge of us. This work demanded more effort, but again there were no German supervisors and there was no pressure. Lilka and I, after getting the tools, would often sneak away into the bushes, lie there until the end of the day and talk and talk and dream about the day of freedom, the day of the Nazis' defeat. To my great regret, for Lilka this was only a dream; later the Nazis murdered her. Most of the time we would lie there until noon and some times even sleep. We needed to be careful that the watchmen, who came from time to time to check on what we were doing, should see us working. We also feared that some German could suddenly appear and catch us among the bushes, in which case it could end badly. For some reason or other we took the risk, and even today I can't understand why. After a month or so we were told that they did not need such a large group of girls, half the number was sufficient. The Polish man came to select the girls that were to stay; unbelievably, Lilka and I were among the ten girls he selected. The girls envied us and attributed my selection to my smile. We were happy to stay there, but it was now impossible to get away into the bushes. After two weeks we completed the work and were not needed there anymore. It had been pleasant there and we so were sorry that the work ended.

We went back to working inside the kibbutz, taking turns being on duty. The situation was not easy for there was little food and it was very cold. Nevertheless, we always had many visitors, not only from *Hashomer-HaTsair*, but also from other youth organizations. Among them were Vatsek Shmulewitz (Halina's

---

[11] Later: chairman of the World Federation of Polish Jews

brother) and a friend of his, both from *HaNoar HaZioni* (Zionist Youth Organization), and also Pola Rapaport (now Lubling). It was Pola who told me that she would occasionally bring coal for heating or a bucket full of potatoes to the kibbutz and would sometimes invite friends for a meal at her home. During this time, until the *Action*[12] in September 1942, life was reasonably quiet. Some shops even remained in Jewish hands. Most of the families in the ghetto were still together. Pola lived with her parents and their conditions were reasonable.

The Friendship with Josek Kantor

One day when I returned to the kibbutz, I saw the girls sitting around in a circle talking with a fellow I didn't know. I joined the circle and then this young man turned his attention to me. At that moment I fell in love with him. I didn't know exactly why, maybe because of his naughtiness, or his infectious laugh, which revealed extremely beautiful teeth, all I know is that it was click and that was that. Never before had I felt like this. He was Josef Kantor, whom everyone called Josek, a fellow of average height, lovely and full of life, four years older than me. He started coming to the kibbutz and from time to time we would go for a walk or for some coffee in a private house. It turned out that he and his girlfriend Mala had ended their relationship a short time before I had arrived in Czestochowa. They were in the same *Gedud* in *Hashomer-HaTsair* and they remained friends. I never asked why they broke up. Josek and I would sometimes visit her. She was a very beautiful and sympathetic girl, the only daughter of elderly parents who helped them earn a living.

I celebrated the *Pesakh Seder* on April 2, 1942 at Josek's home together with his parents and his brother David. His parents were

---

[12] *Action* - every operation the Nazis performed in the Ghettos, most of them connected with sending people to their death.

traditional and the *Seder* was conducted according to tradition. I was quite moved, because I was not used to seeing a complete family anymore, as by then I had not had a family for two and a half years. Our meetings became more frequent and we became friends. Once he didn't appear for a few days and I didn't know what to think, until I found out that the Gestapo had detained him. I was sure that we would not see each other again, but a miracle happened and he was freed. I didn't know why he was detained, but I understood from him that he was involved in some activities for the *Judenrat* and he threatened that he would not remain silent if he were not freed from the Gestapo.

Some time in June or July 1942, Tosia Altman and Aryeh Vilner appeared, each on different days and told us that Jews were being transferred from their homes to an unknown place in crowded freight trains. They were without water in the heat of the summer in terribly unsanitary conditions. Many people, particularly children, died on the long trip to the death camps. They also told us about the systematic extermination of Jews in the death camps. I was shocked and again my mind could not grasp that human beings could carry out such atrocities. In my mind I saw the poor closed-in people choking and traveling to their death. Then and there I made a conscious decision that I would never enter those trains. I would rather be shot instead! I recall that Aryeh Vilner spoke about organizing an underground against the Germans. In fact the kibbutz became a meeting point for the *Shelihim* from Warsaw and other towns and became the regional base of the Jewish Fighters Organization. The *Shelihim* tried to convince the *Judenrat* men to tell the people the truth about the terrible atrocities, so that the people would have no illusions, but the *Judenrat* men refused. They still believed that in Czestochowa there would not be any *Actions*, that in this city there were many arms factories and the Germans would need the Jewish workers. They believed that the special location of the ghetto supported their arguments.

The Great *Action*

Early in the morning of September 22, 1942, the day after *Yom Kippur*, groups of Ukrainians in German service as well as German gendarmes entered the ghetto, stopping beside each house leaving one or two guards. The Gestapo and SS men arrived. At 5:00 AM we heard the shots and the shouts of the Germans. We understood that what we had feared, the *Action*, the *Selection* and deportation of most of the Jews to the death camps, had begun. Jews were ordered to leave their houses street by street, to form lines and move to the market square (The *Rinechek*). The commander of the *Action*, Degenhart, stood with stick in hand, looking at those passing in front of him and sorting them, to the right or to the left. SS men and Ukrainians helped him, while the Jewish police checked that the lines were orderly.

In the kibbutz enormous tension prevailed. There was no possibility of resistance. Our attempts at organizing a resistance had only begun, and in fact we didn't even have one pistol. We also didn't know what was happening outside, we heard shouting and orders, but we were still shut in our flat. Later on we realized that there were actually five consecutive *Actions*, each one being carried out in streets earmarked beforehand. Between each *Action* there was an interval of a few days and every time we hoped that we had been saved and that these episodes had ended. Altogether these *Selections* lasted for two to three weeks.

One day it was our street's turn. We rose early in the morning, dressed in our best garments in order to look well groomed. I recall that I put on a dark blue skirt with a white blouse and on it a training shirt, the collar of the blouse over the collar of the training shirt. Tension was great and we hardly spoke to each other. Everybody was deep in thought, wondering what was in store life or death? We knew that even for those who would survive this time, it would only be a temporary delay, because the Nazis' goal was to murder all Jews. Nevertheless, we prayed for life, even if it was only a postponement of the inevitable, death. We wanted to believe that as long as we lived there was hope and we wanted so much to live! Suddenly Tsiporka Heinsdorf approached me and said: "You should not fear, you will pass the *Selection* and I will not. Why do you say that? I heard that they pass the young." I tried to comfort her as well as myself, but she replied: "That is how I feel."

Shortly afterwards we heard the order to proceed into the street. Our hearts were beating rapidly. We made our way outside, as we had no other choice. We formed lines, six in a line I think, and started to move toward Degenhart and his helpers. Suddenly I heard a Jewish policeman whispering to his relative: "This *Action* is really murderous, much worse than the previous ones (this was the third or the fourth *Action*). Most of the people will be sent to deportation (death), say that you are a seamstress or a furrier." At that moment I decided to say that I was a furrier, because this vocation is even less common than that of a seamstress. We continued moving forward and I tried to understand which side people would be sent for deportation. I saw that most of the people, among them the old and the children, were sent to the right hand side. I realized that this was the side for deportation to the death camps. I decided that if I were sent to the right, I would try to escape, as I had promised myself that I would never enter the trains. I said to my friend Lilka, who was beside me, "Let's go towards the back, in order not to be among the families with the old and the children."

At first I suggested escaping into a nearby house, but she didn't agree, saying that the house was empty and they would certainly search there. I thought that maybe she was right about the house, but I didn't give up on going to the back, until I arrived in a line in which there were young men and I was the only girl. I was able to go there because the guards at the sides were Jewish policemen. I wanted the Germans to see me so that it would be possible for me to tell them that I was a furrier. By and large, except for the young men, they would not stop the people, nor even look at them. Degenhart would only direct them with his stick, to the right. When we arrived before him, the line stopped, and he began to ask the fellows about their vocations. I didn't wait to be asked, fearing that he wouldn't ask at all and would send me straight to the right. With a rapidly beating heart I approached him and said that I was a furrier. The SS man nearby said: "not needed." The fellows started to run to the left and I remained standing there for a few seconds completely confused. It was forbidden to stop and to hold up the line. I made a few steps to the right, wondering how I could escape, and than a miracle happened. Degenhart called me back saying to the SS man: "Perhaps we do need her," and sent me to the left.

The word *miracle* is not the right one to describe what had happened to me. It was *incomprehensible*, and I honestly believe that Divine Providence intervened. Otherwise how can it be explained that Degenhart, the chief of the gendarme and in charge of the ghetto, a murderer who sent people to death by moving his stick, who didn't care for anybody, who shot men, women and children without batting an eyelash - this man called me back? Why? What made him decide to change his mind at this critical moment in my life? The Jewish policeman who saw this all happen hurried me on telling me to "run fast before he regrets it." Thus, most of the boys and I were rescued this time, but to my sorrow, almost none of the girls from the kibbutz survived that *Action*, including Lilka. Only Sarah Vermuth survived that *Action*, because she accidentally happened to be on another street where the *Selection* was more moderate. From about 55,000 to 60,000 Jews (this number came from Krause, who worked in the *Arbeitsamt* in the ghetto) who were in the Great Ghetto during that *Action* on this dreadful day, only 5,000 legal and about 2,000 illegal Jews remained. All the others were sent to their deaths in Treblinka!

The Germans transferred me, and those remaining to the halls of the *Metalurgia* factory in the city. There we were held for a few days until Jewish workers had emptied out all the houses on those streets that had been planned for a new ghetto called, The Small Ghetto. From *Metalurgia* we were transferred to the Small Ghetto, but not before another *Selection*. Elderly people and children who had somehow managed not to be taken during previous *Selections* were deported. Degenhart located most of the so-called illegal people who had managed to hide in different places. He shot some of them on the spot, others he sent to Radomsk and from there to the death camp in Treblinka.

The Small Ghetto

The Small Ghetto was situated in a few old, narrow and dirty streets. It was surrounded by wire fences and guarded by German gendarmes with the help of Polish and Jewish policemen. At one place in the fence, near the *Rinechek* (the small market), there was a gate through which the Jewish workers would go to work. According to a German order, a *Judenrat* was organized, responsible for life in the ghetto. There was a public kitchen, also a laundry, where the inhabitants would hand over their washing. We, the few members of the kibbutz of *Hashomer-HaTsair*, who survived the *Selection* and some local members of the movement, settled down as a kibbutz in a flat at Nadzhechna Street No 71. Through its yard it was possible to pass to Garncharska Street. The members of *Gordonia*[13] and *Dror* lived in another flat in the same house. There I became acquainted with Yehudah Zimerman. In this ghetto I again met Sarah Vermuth and my friend Josek Kantor, who both survived the selection. Meeting them was very exciting because we had had no idea what happened to anyone. Josek lived with his brother David and another fellow in a flat at Nadzhechna Street No 88 where we would meet every day.

Everyone in the Small Ghetto was forced to work, as usual under threat of death. At 6:00 AM groups of workers would leave the

---

[13] *Gordonia, Dror, Hashomer HaTsair* - Zionist Youth organizations

ghetto to go to work, primarily to arms factories such as *Hasag*, *Rakov* and others, guarded by armed Germans, who would sometimes hit them. I worked in a group in the Great Ghetto, which had been totally evacuated where we had to collect and sort the things left behind in the empty flats. Every worker had a ration card for the day, but I don't remember what we were able to get for this card. Coming back from work, the Germans would search the workers from time to time, to make sure that nobody took anything. Woe to the worker if they found something. At best he would be hit, but at worst, shot on the spot. Nevertheless, there were people who took the risk and many of them paid with their lives. Entering the ghetto was nerve racking. I never took anything, not even a pencil, but nonetheless I lived in fear, because I never knew what might happen near the gate. Sometimes they picked people from the lines and sent them to an unknown place. People, who worked in the ghetto, such as in the public kitchen or the laundry or in other necessary jobs, would get special permits to remain in the ghetto during the day. People who worked night shifts received the same permits. As I remember the food was not bad, or completely satisfying, but no one died from hunger. I think that "thefts" from the Great Ghetto helped some people survive.

I don't remember the exact situation in our kibbutz. I only know that we had our own kitchen and that Chesia Borkovsky-Nisky was in charge of it. Most of the people worked; the *Joint* also helped. Inside the kibbutz there were social and underground activities despite the curfew at 8:00 PM. The problem was the unpredictable and scary *Actions*. The Germans would suddenly enter the ghetto and take people from the streets and houses, and usually send them to Treblinka. One of the members, Mendel Fishelewitz who was sent to Treblinka, managed to escape from there and return back to the ghetto. Later, he was one of the first to actively resist the Germans.

One day the Germans gathered all the *intelligentsia* and their families together and told them that they were going to *Eretz-*

Yisrael. Instead they were taken to the Jewish cemetery and they were shot. Degenhart was responsible for all these events. We never knew what the next day would bring, or for that matter, the next hour. In spite of all this we didn't despair. On the contrary, we attempted to live, to love and to be happy during the quiet time. We also saw the reality and looked for ways to survive when possible. We wanted to be able to fight the Germans and to organize against them, although we knew beforehand that we were fighting a losing battle.

In the Underground

In the Great Ghetto there were already talks with Aryeh Vilner (Jurek) about the need to organize resistance against the Germans. This didn't materialize because of what happened afterwards. During the liquidation of the Great Ghetto, some of our members were also sent to Treblinka. The final push to establish the underground was a result of peoples' stories, mainly Fishelewitz, who escaped from there.

Their information concerning the murder of Czestochowa Jews in the gas chambers left no doubt anymore about German intentions. With the encouragement of the *Shelihim* (messengers) from Warsaw, *Hashomer-HaTsair*, *Gordonia* and *Dror* were the first to organize. Later, group "66" joined, their name coming from the fact that they lived as a collective at Nadzhechna Street No 66. Youths, who had belonged to the Zionist organization at one time or another, as well as other groups, joined the underground later. All organized under an umbrella organization called *ZOB* (*Zydowska Organizacja Bojowa* -The Jewish Fighters Organization). First headquarter members were Bolek Gevirtzman and Yehudah Glikstein from *Hashomer-HaTsair*, Rivkah Glantz from *Dror*, the contact between the *ZOB* and Warsaw and other cities. Mietek Ferleger from the "66" group was responsible for purchasing arms and Somek Abramowitz from the Communists was responsible for maintaining contact with the Polish underground.

Moitek Zilberberg (born in Kalish) was elected as the commander. He was older than us and had military experience as a former soldier in the Polish Army. He was a serious man with organizational abilities. Later Fishelewitz and Tsevi (Yatsek) Viernik also joined the leadership and were responsible for producing the explosives and grenades. The raw materials were stolen from the Germans. My boyfriend Josek joined the leadership and he was responsible for the administration of the organization. He was in charge of collecting money from the wealthy to buy arms, as well as building bunkers and tunnels, which led outside the Small Ghetto. Up to 100 people participated.

For the first time the question of how to actually carry out the idea of resistance arose: Should the struggle be only in the ghetto or also in the woods where members would go? It was finally decided that there would be active resistance inside the ghetto, sabotage acts outside the ghetto and partisan activities in the woods.

To fulfill all these tasks a large quantity of arms were required and these were very expensive. We obtained the money after persuading the wealthy. If this didn't work assigned members would take the wealthy into a cellar and keep them there until their families agreed to support our activities. There were Polish looking members whose job it was to buy arms outside the ghetto, a very difficult task. The Poles didn't want to sell and if they agreed they demanded a large amount of money. Often they cheated our people by selling them faulty arms or informing on them to the Germans.

משרד הביטחון
אגף כוח אדם

* 2839 -

שם משפחה   בויקו

שם פרטי   פנינה (פולה)

שם האב   אליעזר

מס' זהות   633772

בזה ניתנת לך הזכות
לענידת
אות הלוחם בנאצים

י. עמיר
ראש אגף כוח אדם
יו"ר הועדה

כ"ז ניסן תשכ"ז 7 באפ' 1967

העיטור מוענק כאות הערכה
על פועלך במלחמה נגד הנאצים
במלחמת העולם השניה

משרד הביטחון

The Israel Ministry of Defense presented the "Fighters Against the Nazis" medal to Peninah.

(Photo taken by Tsevi Viernik)

A meeting of a group of former members of the Czestochowa Underground in Tel Aviv in the summer of 1995

From left: Josef (guest), Aryeh Gutkind, Sarka Adelist, Peninah, Adam Shteinbrekher, Chesha Eikhenvald, Franka Kozlovska, Pola Rapoport, Bolek Gevirtsman

The Action of January 4, 1943

On the morning of January 4th, when the underground was still in its infancy, Germans surrounded the ghetto and forced the habitants to gather in the Small Market Square *(Rinetchek)*, near the fence outside the ghetto. This *Action* surprised us, coming at a moment when most of the underground members were working outside the ghetto. About 12 to 15 people inside the ghetto including me gathered in the attic of a house and decided that as a first act of resistance we would not go to the square. After further discussion we decided that it was no use to sit and wait until the Germans came and killed us all, but rather to go out and kill the heads of the selection. The truth was that only Fishelevitz had a pistol and Izho Feiner (Paya) a knife, and a few girls had hand tools. We left the attic to go to the square, but the ghetto streets were empty except for Germans. When they saw us they immediately directed us to deportation apparently to Treblinka as a punishment for not appearing on time. I stood in line overcome with fear as I thought about the wagons and the gas chambers and decided to escape. Better to be shot instead. At that moment Fishelevitz drew his pistol intending to shoot the German officer, but unfortunately the pistol failed to fire, as it was faulty. He stayed calm, attacked the German and knocked him down to the ground. Feiner attacked another officer with his knife and injured him. Both were immediately shot. Tumult broke out, the Germans didn't know what was happening and became frightened. I didn't think much, but took advantage of the disorder and escaped from the square.

Saved for a Second Time

I escaped, but where to go? I didn't know the area or anyone I could go to. Nearby, I saw a half-ruined house, and I entered it. The house was empty. Using a ladder I climbed to the second floor pulling the ladder up behind me to prevent anyone else from climbing up. Through a crack in the wall opposite the square I saw the Germans, by now recovered from the shock, taking every tenth man out of the line and shooting him on the spot. They murdered 27 men, among them Viernik's brother. The house was so close to the square that I could hear the Germans telling the policemen that many Jews had escaped and that it was imperative to find them. I sat down in a corner behind a half - broken door and took hold of a big stone I found there. I thought if somebody found me I would throw the stone at him in order to be shot anything to avoid entering the trains! After awhile I decided to look for a better hideout. It was cold and everything was covered with snow. I looked through the ruined wall at the rear of the house and it seemed that near the house, at the hidden side from the square, there was a pit in which I could hide. I jumped down nearly one floor, but then realized that my eyes had deceived me, for there was no pit, only a great plot covered by a snow pile with a street at its end. I was at a loss, but finally decided to walk parallel to the fence of the ghetto, keeping away from the square. I also wanted to avoid the Poles who could hand me over to the Gestapo. Walking on in my chosen direction, a Pole suddenly appeared in front of me, and when passing beside me without stopping whispered to me: "Don't go in this direction, the Germans killed a woman and her daughter there not long ago." I don't know why, but I believed him and it was as though an "Angel from Heaven" had appeared to warn me. I started to go through the empty snowy plot in the direction of the street I had seen before thinking that I would enter some backyard and hide in a W.C.[14] until evening and then find one of the working groups returning to the ghetto and join it. Actually I didn't know where to look for the Jewish places of work or how to find them, but at that moment my mind was only concerned with where to hide.

Before I reached the street I removed the stripe with the *Magen-David* from my sleeve hoping not to be recognized as a Jew. On the street I saw two young Poles who were standing there as though they were waiting for me and they asked me: "What is happening there in the ghetto?" I understood that it was pointless to pretend that I was not Jewish, so I told them about the *Action* and that I had escaped and asked them if they could hide me until evening. They suggested that they would look for a cart, take me to a village for a week and then bring me back to the ghetto. I had no faith in them, and when they appeared to be looking for the cart, I ran away. I went into a W.C. in a backyard and waited there for almost an hour. Looking back I think that if those youngsters had wanted to hand me over to the Gestapo, one of them would have stayed to watch over me, but it seems to me that they simply didn't know what to do with me. I stepped out of the W.C. It was about 3:00 PM. I started to go back through the snowy field towards the ghetto. Suddenly I saw a

---

[14] W.C. water closet - in these times most of the toilets were in the backyards and not in the flats

group of people, children and adults, walking on the same path toward me. I thought that the children would soon start to shout "Jew" and then I would be found out. I was scared and turned around and stepped down to the side off the path. Suddenly, I felt somebody walking quickly behind me and started to go faster, but the man reached me and I heard him say: "Get back onto the path, otherwise people will realize that you are a stranger here." After this he asked me what was going on. I told him the truth and asked if he could hide me until evening when the Jews returned from their work places back to the ghetto. I would then return with them. He said he couldn't, but would ask one of the women in the group to help me. It turned out that they were workers returning home from the factories they worked in. The group came nearer and the man approached a woman, I think her name was Kachkowska, asking her to take me to her home for a few hours. She hesitated out of fear, but agreed after I pleaded with her. Her fear was understandable because if the Germans were to find me in her home all of us would be shot. When I sat down in her home, after hours of rushing around with enormous tension, I started to cry. I cried and cried and this good woman tried to calm me: "Don't cry, everything will be all right" she said, and she brought me a bowl of hot soup. I was frozen and the soup helped warm me and relax me a little. Then I saw her daughter, a nice girl named Vanda, about my age, full of joy, dressed to go to the cinema. How I envied her! I thought, "Oh God, what sin have I committed that I am sitting here miserable." My life is endangered and that girl, a human being just like me, has the right to live and I do not. Meanwhile curious neighbors came to look at me. I became a little frightened and the hostess felt it and said: "You should not be afraid, no one here will betray you."

At 5:00 PM a group of Jews was supposed to finish work at some plant. At 4:30 PM my hostess brought a young fellow named Jashek who would escort me to the working group with whom I would then enter the ghetto. Before we parted, I offered her money, but she refused to take any. Instead she asked me to buy butter from her and to bring her a suitcase through Jews she was working with. She gave me a small note with her name and her place of work. I promised I would do so, not thinking at that moment that it was impossible to pass a suitcase through the ghetto gate. Even if I could somehow get it in, there were no shops in the ghetto. My thoughts at that moment were apparently somewhere else. I bought the butter and paid much more than she had asked. I thanked her with all my heart for her indispensable help in my desperate situation and went out with Jashek to meet the Jewish workers. Outside it was almost dark as he went into the factory to check out the situation. He came back with the bad news telling me that the group had left an hour earlier due to the events in the ghetto. He tried to comfort me saying that there was a second shift that would finish work at 10:00 PM. I was shocked and didn't know what to do when Jashek proposed that we return to the woman and wait there until 10:00 PM. Returning to the woman I saw that she was frightened, but she didn't say anything. We sat and talked, but I felt the tension in the air. I was tense too. When it was finally 8:00 PM, I suggested to Jashek that perhaps we should go now, as maybe this group would also leave early. I thanked my hostess again and we left.

Jashek was a nice sympathetic fellow, a little older then me and quite good-hearted, otherwise why would he accompany me from 4:00 PM until 10:00 PM and endanger himself by twice going with me to Mrs. Kachkowska not leaving me until he saw me safely join the group. Truly, I don't know what I would have done without him. We talked a lot and I learned that the majority of people living in the neighborhood like him were members of the Socialist Party. We waited for an hour and a half until the group finished working. Before I joined their lines, we parted warmly and with a kiss and the wish that the war would end quickly with the defeat of the Germans and he added: "Stand firm!"

It turned out that the people in this work group already knew that somebody would join them. My friends in the ghetto also knew that I was safe. Coming back, Josek and a few of my girlfriends were waiting for me by the gate. When I came to the kibbutz, I suddenly felt that I couldn't walk. As a result of the enormous emotion and tension I lost my ability to walk. For two weeks I lay in bed. During this time, I have no idea how it happened, I lost the small note from my savior and worse yet I forgot her name. I just blocked out her name in my memory and was totally unable to recall it. After the war, my friend Sabka Bornstein (who became Susan Ostrowitz, and who was born in Czestochowa) and I attempted to find her. We searched the street where according to my memory the woman's house should have been. I thought that if I saw it maybe I would recognize it, but I didn't. Susan said that there was no reason to look for somebody without at least having an address. Only after many years the names "Kachkowska, Vanda and Jashek" came back to me. Sometimes I think about them and cannot forgive myself for losing the note as it might have given me the opportunity to see them again and to thank them properly. Perhaps I would have met the man who ran after me cautioning me not to trample in the snow. He told me to walk on the path and tried so hard to find shelter for me, even if it was only for a few hours. In the end it was these people who ultimately helped save my life.

Back in the Ghetto

Coming back to the ghetto I often thought how lucky I had been to meet these wonderful people, who I believe, were sent by Providence at exactly the right moment. Most of the girls who were with me in the attic were sent to the trains. A few of them jumped from them and were shot to death and one committed suicide. A few of the girls jumped and remained uninjured, amongst them Chesia Borkowska and my friend Sarah Vermut who was murdered later, during the liquidation of the Small Ghetto.

Left: Josek (Josef) Kantor, my spouse in the Czestochowa ghetto. The Germans shot Josek during the liquidation of the underground.

Right: David Kantor, Josek's brother. The Nazis murdered him during a death march.

Once I recovered, Josek and I decided to formalize our relationship. In spite of the situation we lived in and despite the fact that we felt our lives were worthless, we married. We were young and we dared to dream. We dared to hope about better times to come. I believe that there was no rabbi in the ghetto, so instead we had a civil marriage. We were registered in one of the offices of the *Judenrat* and I received a new certificate with the name of Pola Kantor. My friends from the underground know me by this name even today. I left the kibbutz and moved to Josek's two-room flat at Nadzhechna Street No 88. Thanks to Josek I didn't work outside the ghetto any longer. I was able to get a permit from a senior official of the *Arbeitseinsatz* (Employment

Bureau), Moshe (Mazhey) Krause, who was also a member of the Underground and a good friend of Josek's. The permit certified that I was working inside the ghetto. He also supplied permits for other members of the underground whose activities required them to be inside the ghetto. About this time I obtained a capsule of cyanide[15] enveloped in wax. Maybe this seems strange, but this capsule gave me a feeling of confidence that my life didn't depend on the Germans. I kept it and looked after it, for it was very significant to me to have the option to use it.

After January 4th the underground activity accelerated. Two central bunkers (a subterranean hiding place) were built at Garncharska Street No 40 and Nadzhechna Street No 88; the latter served also as the central stockroom of the headquarters. Subterranean passages to the Polish side were excavated from those two bunkers, so that the fighters could escape to the woods, if and when needed. One or two more bunkers were built, but without the subterranean passages to the Polish side. The excavation of the passages was usually done at night; a group of us would stay outside to warn the diggers of possible danger ahead. The entrances to the bunkers and the passages were camouflaged. It was very hard work, all done by crawling back and forth. Josek was in charge of the building of the bunkers and the passages and had about 100 people under his command. The bunker at Nadzhechna Street was built in the cellar of the house in which we lived. The entrance to the tunnel was through an oven on the first floor. We lived on the second floor together with Josek's brother David and another fellow, Silver, both members of the underground. The underground also organized an intelligence unit that gathered information about German intentions in the ghetto, discovered traitors and informers, and kept contact with Warsaw and the Polish underground. Other groups were being trained in the use of arms and in sabotage. The arms situation had improved enormously after January 4th.

---

[15] Cyanide - a very strong poison

Many pistols had been bought (I don't remember if there were any rifles) along with a large number of Molotov cocktails and grenades, which Tsevi Viernik and the inventor of the process, Shlamek Koifman and their comrades, managed to produce. We also obtained uniforms of German Army (*Wehrmacht*) and the Security Police (*Sicherheits Polizei*) as well as military boots and other items. All this was stored in the central bunker of Nadzhechna No 88. Gunpowder and other explosives were kept in the Garncharska No 40 bunker.

One of the underground operations that failed was meant to damage the railway system near the city. To get to the planned site, the boys joined a working group that was leaving the ghetto, but unfortunately the German guards saw them disappearing from the lines and shot them. Two were murdered on the spot; two managed to escape and one, Tsevi Lustiger was injured and caught. He was severely tortured to make him divulge who had sent him and who was the commander of the organization, but Tsevi behaved like a hero and didn't reveal a word. I knew him well because he and I were both members of the kibbutz. He was a gentle, shy boy.

Two positions were established under the leadership of Bolek Gevirtsman (Ben-Ya'akov) in the woods *Zloty Potok* and *Konitspol*. These positions, except for partisan activities were meant to serve as a base for the underground members in case of the liquidation of the ghetto as well as a meeting place with the Polish partisans. The Poles, who were supposed to help, didn't appear, and the groups who arrived there, suffered great losses, largely from the Polish anti-Semitic bands, which traveled into the villages and murdered Jews.

My Life in the Small Ghetto

Three things affected my life in the ghetto: my role as a housewife, membership in the underground and the fear of *Actions*. As a housewife I lived more or less a normal life cooking and keeping our room in order, etc. We had one room; David and Silver had the other. David's attitude towards me was very friendly and he accepted me willingly in the small flat. As a member of the underground my main job was to be watching outside when the boys were digging the bunkers and passages. Josek was among the activists so people often came to us to discuss different problems. Rivkah Glantz would often be a guest at our house; she was a *Kasharith* (young girl who maintained communications between the Jewish underground groups) from Warsaw, who was among the founders of the underground in Czestochowa and at the beginning a member of its headquarters. As a result, I was unintentionally kept up to date, at least as regards some of the events. The third thing seriously affecting my life was the fear of the *Actions*. When a German SS man entered the ghetto everything looked different and took on significance. Suddenly you realized that maybe in a few moments or hours you would be dead. Being so young, I wanted to live. In times of relative quiet I tried not to think about the cruel reality and to live my life as normally as possible in order not to go crazy thinking about the precariousness of my life.

After the *Action* of January 4th there was another one on March 21st. The Germans again took people from their houses or off the streets and sent most of them to Treblinka. A few of the members of our kibbutz were also taken and in these cases the arrests were made according to lists the German had.

On May 1, 1943 the Germans closed the ghetto and nobody went to work outside. The headquarters of the underground declared a state of alarm assuming that the liquidation of the ghetto was about to take place. Arms were distributed to the members and they were sent to previously planned posts. The tension lasted for three days, but nothing happened. It turned out that these were precautionary measures taken by the Germans on May 1st the workers' holiday, and May 3rd the Polish national holiday.

In June, Gestapo visits to the ghetto became more frequent as they seemed to be trying to find out what was going on inside the ghetto. One day, about a week before its liquidation, one of the ghetto members asked me if I would be prepared to carry a pistol and a grenade from the central bunker to the bunker at Mostowa Street. Without much thought I agreed. I took my wickerwork basket, put the pistol and grenade in it and covered them with my sky blue nightgown (its strange that I still remember the color), and went outside. It was around six or seven at night, and there were no people in the street. I had gone a fair distance, when suddenly I saw one of the Germans coming toward me. My first impulse was to turn back, but something stopped me. "No," I thought, this would arouse his suspicion and I decided to go toward him. I tried to pass him with self-confidence and a smile and he didn't stop me. I was very anxious that he was following me, but I was afraid to look back. Only after a few minutes, when I didn't hear any footsteps behind me, I dared to turn around. When I saw that everything was all right I began to tremble and could hardly continue thinking how lucky I was, yet again. Until this day, the thought of what could have happened to me, if he had searched me, makes me ill. It wasn't only the fear of death, but more so the Gestapo interrogation.

The Liquidation of the Small Ghetto and the Death of Josek

On June 25, 1943, Germans surrounded the ghetto. This was preceded by two weeks of tension, alarms and standbys in the underground. On that morning a standby and call up of the members had also been declared. About 40 people gathered in the central bunker at Nadzhechna No 88. The plan, according to Avraham Zilberstein, member of the Kibbutz *Ma'apilim* of *Hashomer-HaTsair*, and an active member of the underground, was that in case of an *Action* or detection of the bunker, the

Germans were to be stopped by throwing a grenade at them. At the same time we were to get into the passage and crawl through the tunnel to its exit at the Polish side of the town that was camouflaged in a deserted shop of light drinks near the house of the German sentry post. We were to then attack the post by taking the sentries guns, and breaking through into the ghetto from the outside, setting fire to everything possible and urging the ghetto population to escape. We would then continue to our location in the woods of *Konitspol* where a group of partisans were already located. Outside the bunker a few members stood guard at lookout posts and they had to inform us periodically about what was going on inside the ghetto.

Suddenly, at about 10:00 AM, we heard footsteps and knocks at the door above. It was clear the Germans were looking for the entrance to the bunker. Tension was great and we waited to see what the Germans' next step would be, but then at 11:00 AM it became quiet. Our guards reported that the workers from the nightshift had entered the ghetto, the dayshift went out to work, and that the Germans had left. We were relieved and waited until 1:30 PM, at which time the standby state was cancelled. The members handed over their arms and started to leave the bunker. Only Moitek, the commander who was ill, stayed together with Lutek Glikstein who was looking after him. Josek and I went up to our flat and Josek decided to go out for a haircut. I stayed at home and prepared lunch (David and Silver were not at home). I stood in the kitchen near the window peeling potatoes when suddenly I felt an urge to look outside. A big car had stopped near our house and Germans were jumping from it. I realized immediately that I had to escape from this house where the central bunker was situated and which was now surrounded by SS men. I was glad that Josek wasn't at home and that the barbershop was quite far from here. I threw the knife away, took my coat and ran from the flat. As I ran down the stairs I saw Josek standing on the first floor speaking with Shildhaus. I shouted "Germans!" There was no chance of entering the bunker, so the three of us left the house through the back and ran along the fence of the ghetto. The German guards outside the ghetto, who were watching so that nobody could escape, didn't shoot at us. We didn't go far and for some unknown reason the boys entered a house and I followed. In fact, the aim was to run to another bunker, but maybe because of the great distance to that bunker and the shooting we heard in the street, they entered the aforementioned house. The moment we entered it I knew that it was not a safe place. It was too close to the central bunker that was surrounded by the Germans. I suggested we leave. We consulted and after a short while it was decided that I would go into the street to see what was happening. They thought that as a girl I stood a better chance of not being detained. Before I went out Josek gave me some money and said: "If you survive and I don't, and you get to *Eretz-Yisrael*, look for my sister Esther Shildhaus, who lives in Tel Aviv and introduce yourself to her, since you are my wife." I went out into the street and soon two Germans from the Gestapo or the Security Police came towards me, but they didn't stop me. The boy who went ahead of me was stopped and asked to show a certificate. When I passed them I heard him saying the name "Miska" and explaining something. I don't know why they didn't stop me, maybe because I was a girl or because they were busy with the boy and didn't pay attention to me. I wanted to go to the kibbutz flat, where I thought that maybe I could get certificates with other names for Josek, Shildhaus and me. I feared that the Germans not only knew the places of the bunkers, but also the names of the underground members. On my way to the kibbutz I met Uta. She asked where I was going and why. She embraced me and said that there was no point going back because the Germans had murdered everybody, men and women who were in the house of the central bunker and in the houses nearby. Among the victims were Josek and Shildhaus. I started to cry. I felt a burning ache and I felt absolutely helpless. Only about ten minutes had passed from the moment I left them and the cursed Germans had already succeeded in killing them. I was shocked and didn't know what to do as I couldn't help Josek anymore. (An eyewitness told me that before the German shot him, Josek spat in his face).

Finally I decided to continue to the kibbutz and to hear what had been decided there. On arrival I found the flat empty. Suddenly a girl, whose name I have forgotten, came in and asked me to lend her my summer coat because she was suffering from heat in her winter coat. She wanted to go and look for the members. On her way back she promised to return my coat and in the meantime, she left hers with me. I agreed, but I never saw either the girl or the coat again. Later on I didn't regret the exchange, although her coat was a little shabby, but it was made from black cloth lined with cotton and in winter, in the *Hasag* camp, it also served as a blanket for me. I waited there for about an hour and when the girl didn't return and other members also didn't appear, I put on the coat and went out to look for them. It was dark and no more shots could be heard. I thought of going to the other bunker at Garncharska Street, when I met Jatsek - Tsevi Viernik, one of the heads of the underground in the ghetto and the manufacturer of the grenades. He asked me where I was going and I told him that I was looking for members of the kibbutz who might be in the other bunker. He told me that they were indeed in that bunker, had tried to leave through the passage to the outside of the ghetto to reach the woods in Konitspol, but the Germans had waited for them near the exit. The underground members had some weapons; there was a battle and almost all of the underground members were murdered. After the war I learned that only a few survived, including Avraham Zilberstein. Jatsek convinced me that after those events there was no point in going to the other bunker because the Germans had probably surrounded the place. He suggested going to another bunker that had no subterranean passage that the Germans possibly didn't know about. When we arrived a few people were already gathered there. According to Jatsek, this bunker served as a storeroom for explosives. We sat there until the morning not knowing what awaited us. We were glad that we had explosives to use if the Germans found us. Nobody slept that night.

We knew that there were informers among the Jews in the ghetto and some of them were executed. It was also clear that there was an informer in the underground who provided the Germans with maps of the bunkers and the names of some underground members. Among the informers there was a Jew who worked with the Germans at the guardroom near the entrance to the ghetto; he was the one who guided the Germans to the central bunker at Nadzhechna No 88. His collaboration with the Germans became known only a few days before the liquidation of the Small Ghetto. I didn't know why he wasn't immediately executed nor do I know if he was executed at all.

As I stated previously, Moitek Zilberberg, the commander who was ill, and Lutek Glikstein stayed in the central bunker. There were two versions of Moitek's death: one that he committed suicide swallowing the cyanide capsule in his possession and the second version that he died from a German bullet during the fight. Lutek managed to escape through the passage that had several exits. He reached the Konitspol woods and was killed there in a partisan activity. The Germans removed everything from the bunker including the arms, a big quantity of food, medication, German uniforms etc., all of which had been accumulated with much effort and great danger. Thus with great cunning the Germans succeeded in neutralizing our ghetto resistance.

The Camp at *Hasag*

The next morning the Jewish Police ordered all inhabitants of the Small Ghetto to gather at the *Rinechek* square, promising them that all would be sent to work at the *Hasag* factory in Czestochowa. Anybody found in the ghetto thereafter would be shot or burned. Having no choice we all went to the *Rinechek,* but the Germans, as usual, didn't keep their promise and instead made a *Selection.*

They picked people from the lines mainly those whom they knew had lived near the central bunker and others. The Germans took them to the Jewish cemetery and murdered them.

Among the people who were shot was Helenka Tenebaum, a beautiful woman in her late twenties who was Degenhart's lover. He arranged for her to live in a nice flat with all possible luxury near the ghetto gate and he would spend most of his free time with her. No one was allowed to visit her except her close friend Stella. People in the ghetto were sure that she would survive, but Degenhart thought otherwise. He sent one of his men to shoot her and her friend in the back. After the war Degenhardt was sentenced to life imprisonment by a court in Lueneburg (Germany) for shooting 51 Jews.

I don't clearly remember what happened to us later. I was tired and upset by the events of the last 24 hours as well as Josek's death. According to my friends' stories, we were led on foot to a factory building and were put in a big hall with scattered straw on its floor where we lived in very crowded conditions for a few days. After that we were led into barracks near the *Hasag* factory. A barbed wire fence surrounded the factory. Men and women had separate barracks, but on the same site and not far from each other, so after work we were able to meet.

The monument in memory of the Czestochowa Jewish fighters who fell in battle against the Nazis.

The condition in Hasag, compared to other camps, was better. We were able to manage unless there were *Actions* causing fear. During the first months in *Hasag* there were frequent *Actions* (*Selections*), which meant death for those who were picked out from the lines. On July 20, 1943, the Germans took the Jewish policemen and their families to the Jewish cemetery and shot them all, as they no longer needed them. Later on people were selected and sent to other work camps, all worse than *Hasag*; but neither we, nor those chosen, knew anything about their destiny. Only after the war, when meeting some of these people, did they tell me about their hardships. In *Hasag* it was important not to go against discipline to prevent being flogged in the guardroom. My friend Genia, now a member of the Kibbutz Givath-HaSheloshah, was late for a parade and received 25 strokes.

A small section of *Hasag camp*

In the barracks there were three tiered bunks. Each floor had one long line of bunks and on each bunk there was a mattress 60 centimeters (two feet) wide filled with straw, one mattress for each person. We didn't have blankets and covered ourselves with our coats. In the middle of the barrack there was an oven used for heating in winter and there were girls who even cooked on it. Our food included 250 grams (about 9 ounces) of bread per day and thin soup for lunch. Once a week we were given a little sugar or jam and from time to time even an egg. All this was luxurious compared to other camps, but it was not sufficient and people who had no money to supplement their food went hungry. I had some money from Josek with which I would buy bread and onions from the Poles who worked together with us in *Hasag*, as an addition to our rations. Later members of the underground, I among them, received money from time to time that arrived by various and strange ways from Switzerland. Tsevi Viernik would receive the money at his working place, *Rakov* (an ammunition factory), by means of a Pole and would transfer part of it to his wife Nacha in *Hasag*, which she then divided among the members.

The director of *Hasag* was considered a more or less decent man. People related later on that when the SS (or the Gestapo) brought us to this place, they demanded that we wear pajamas with stripes like in the other camps, but the director disapproved very vigorously, saying that he was directing a factory, not a zoo. We also didn't get strange identification marks, but a small tin disk similar to the soldiers, where our personal number was engraved, threaded onto a cord and hung around our neck. Cleanliness in the camp, at least in our barracks, was more or less reasonable. In this camp there was a big building with showers and warm water where we could wash every day. Nearby, there was a smaller building with an open lavatory without partitions, consisting of a long bench of concrete with a hole every meter. Here too cleanliness was satisfactory. From time to time the barracks and our clothes were disinfected. In contrast my friends Halina Shmulewitz-Barkani and Pola Rapoport-Lubling told me that there were bed bugs and lice in their barracks and on them. Some inmates contracted typhus and other illnesses and some died. There was even a clinic in the camp with a doctor and a nurse, although it had insufficient means. I never visited it, being lucky not to need it.

While in the camp I met Sabka Bornstein (later Susan Ostrowitz), a nice blond girl, a native of Czestochowa, and we became very good friends. We would eat together and I would share the bread and onions I had bought with her and she shared her blanket with me that she found somewhere. Her mattress was next to mine, so we made partitions from cardboard around them (where we took the cardboard from, I don't remember), leaving the front side open. Most of the girls did the same and this gave us a feeling of privacy. It surprised me then that the *Werkschutz* (the guard of the factory) came to inspect the barracks, he didn't object to those rooms. It was, of course impossible to stand in such a room, but we could sit quite comfortably and even guests would come to visit us. After work we could move around in the camp almost freely, until the allotted hour when we had to be back in the barracks. SS or Gestapo men usually did not enter the camp, but if they came, we knew that something bad was going to happen and we would quickly run to the barracks The men responsible for the barracks, their order and cleanliness, were the *Werkschutz*, who were mostly Ukrainians or *Volksdeutsche* (Germans by nationality who lived outside Germany). One day I did something foolish and until this day I haven't understood how a careful and quite cowardly girl like myself could do such a thing. The *Werkschutz* man Shtiglis, a very wicked individual, entered our barracks to check if the lights were out. He was in a high mood and joked with the girls. I responded to his gaiety and not thinking much put my fingers in my mouth and whistled firmly. He raised his voice, asking who had whistled. It became dead quiet, and no one answered. I had butterflies in my stomach and became very scared. Luckily for me, the lights were turned off and for some reason he didn't persist on getting an answer and my stupidity ended without punishment. It could have cost me a beating on my buttocks or even worse.

The Work at *Hasag*

Hasag was a factory of arms responsible for renewing different kinds of cartridges of ammunition. More than fifty years have passed since then, so it is difficult for me to precisely describe the different departments in the factory. I can remember that there was a *Waescherei*, where the used cartridges were washed; *Lakernia*, where they were coated with varnish; *Infantry,* I can't recall what was done there; *Rekalibrierung*, where the diameters of the used cartridges were checked. I worked in this department during most of the time I was in *Hasag* and it was one of the best departments to work in. At first I worked in the factory yard, gathering and sorting different items scattered there. It was not hard work, but not pleasant either, as most of the time I worked bowed down to the ground and under the supervision of the Jewish foreman. Although it was summer, I remember that my hands were cold. After about two weeks I was transferred to the

Rekalibrierung. I didn't know why, maybe it was simply because the work outside had ended. In my department there were two units: in one unit cartridges of about 10 to 12 cm long were cleaned on the inside and then sent to other departments for further treatment. In the second unit renewed rifle cartridges were finally checked. Both units were in the same hall with no partitions, only a small distance from each other. At the end of the hall there was the office of the *Meister*, the boss. At first, I worked in the cleaning unit. There were machines for cleaning the cartridges from inside by means of rotating brushes. I would hold the cartridge in my hand and put it on the rotating brushes. This work was a little harder than outside in the yard, but its advantage was that we worked in an "air-conditioned" hall, meaning that in summer there were ventilators, and in winter there were radiators along the walls that heated the hall. The work was done sitting down, not standing up, and there were even normal lavatories with seats and doors. Two girls worked at one table and we could chat when the overseers weren't looking. There also were drawbacks. The machines were very noisy and until we were used to it, we could hardly hear each other. During the cleaning a lot of dust was produced. A lack of caution could cause one's hair to be entangled in the rotating brushes and this was very dangerous. I worked at those machines for a few months and was then transferred to the second unit. The work there could have been quite pleasant if not for the fact that we were in a work camp, where there were no human rights and where we knew that our lives were not worth very much. In this unit two or three girls sat at a table and everyone had a different measurement device. One of the chaps who worked there would bring a box of cartridges and put it on the right hand side of the table. We would examine them one by one and we would put the checked ones for use into an empty box at the left side of the table and the disqualified ones we would put into another box. This work demanded absolute cleanliness of the table and hands so we worked with white glove that were changed every day. The work was performed in two shifts and we were divided into two groups, one group working for a week from 6:00 AM until 6:00 PM and the other from 6:00 PM until 6:00 AM and then it would be reversed. Our group was lucky because its German *Meister* was a nice man about 45-50 years of age, a father of two little children. He had lived most of his life in the United States. At the beginning of the war he was expelled back to Germany (about which he was angry) and we called him "the American." He was a good man and almost never sent anyone to be flogged. He also didn't believe or didn't want to believe, in the existence of "Death Camps." Most of the time he would sit in his office and sometimes take a nap at night. In addition to him there was an overseer, a German woman, whom we called *Marchefka* (carrot). She was more or less okay. The other group had an overseer whom we called *"Pietrushka"(*parsley), a real witch. If you did anything she didn't like she would send you to the guardroom to be flogged. We were afraid when she sometimes changed shifts with the *Marchefka*. Then there was a Jewish *Kapo* named Irka, who was not the kind of person people talked about in the Death Camps. As a foreman she never denounced or hit anybody, but there were people who were angry with her and claimed she was responsible for their being sent to other work camps, which were much worse than *Hasag*. I didn't know if this was true. Susan and I were friendly with her and after liberation we lived together in one flat until I left for *Eretz-Yisrael*. People should not think that *Hasag* was a rest home. In other departments the situation was not like in the *Rekalibrierung*. Most of the people there worked hard. For example, Halina told us about *Lakernia* where she worked, or Pola who told us about the *Infantry* where people were not only worked very hard, but were also beaten and abused by the German *Meisters*.

I preferred to work the night shift, from 6:00 PM until 6:00 AM. First of all I did not have to get up for the lineup at 5:30 AM. Latecomers would be in danger of flogging, sometimes even death. I witnessed the killing of a man because he was not in line on time. This depended on the man who took the salute. Also most of the Germans and the *Werkschutz* were asleep at night, so that nighttime was quiet and there was more freedom. We would visit each other at the tables, exchange information about the situation and also tell jokes, mostly macabre. During the night we would also launder our clothes and underwear in the lavatory and hang them onto the radiators to dry, Our *Meister* didn't object, but he warned us that nobody else should see it. Actually there was an *Obermeister* in charge of him and he feared him. When going for a walk or to work we carried our shabby property with us. I had a cardboard box with a handle made of cord. It was about 30 by 40 cm wide (12 by 16 inches) and 20 to 25 cm (8 to 10 inches) high and it was large enough to hold my few clothes and the bread I had.

At the end of work at 6:00 AM we would go to sleep in the barracks. Susan and I would sleep until 12:00 PM when soup was brought and after eating we would go back to sleep until 3 PM or 4 PM. Later in the afternoon we'd go outside to meet people. One day Susan met an acquaintance of hers named Natek (Nathan), who was with another fellow. Natek introduced him as Danek Miska. I recognized the name as soon as I heard it. The Germans had stopped Danek when I passed beside them on the day of the liquidation of the ghetto and Josek's death. Maybe that unknowingly had saved my life. When I asked him how it happened that the Germans had allowed him to pass, he explained that he had a gravedigger's license. From that day the four of us met often when circumstances permitted. We would walk in the confines of the camp or they would come to our barracks. Officially it was forbidden for men to enter women's barracks, but during evening hours there were usually no guards in the area. If guards came we had an agreed upon signal and all the men would go outside. We spent most of our free time with Danek and Natek. We would walk, chat and on warm evenings find some junk to sit on. In time the friendships deepened, and despite the fact that we four were always together, Susan became closer to Natek and I to Danek. Both came from Czestochowa.

We didn't talk about the future, because we didn't believe that there was a future, although by now it was already 1944 and there was news that the Germans were being defeated on several fronts. But there was also information that the Germans would burn the barracks with their inhabitants when they were forced to retreat or take the people with them to Germany. To remain strong we had to have a glimmer of hope, to believe in a miracle. For people who, thank God, have not experienced such conditions, it is difficult to understand our mood.

In addition to *Hasag*, there were a few more work camps in Czestochowa near the arms factories of *Rakov* and Chenstochowianka-Varta. During the liquidation of the Small Ghetto some people including members of the underground, were taken to those camps. There was regular contact between inmates of *Hasag* and *Rakov* via Poles, mainly members of the Polish Socialist Party. One or two of them were close to the leaders of the underground and would transfer the money and letters we received. David Kantor, Josek's brother, was in *Rakov*. At first I didn't know what had happened to him. When the Germans surrounded our house he was not at home. I also didn't see him later in the ghetto and or the *Rinechek*. I thought that the Germans had murdered him or that he had gone to work in the morning and stayed there together with the group. The Germans were very sophisticated and full of guile. To prevent the resistance from the underground and other supporters, they would leave the groups who worked the night shift at their working places and send the groups from the day shift to work. With fewer people in the ghetto the possibility of organizing became less likely. I think that later on those groups were also brought to the *Rinechek* for *Selection*.

In *Hasag* I learned that David was in *Rakov*. After a short time I received a letter from him in which he suggested that I come over to *Rakov*, where in his opinion, the situation was better. (I had no idea how he would get me there.) I thought about his proposal and rejected it, as I didn't want to be obligated to him. I already knew the camp I was in and the conditions in *Hasag*, and I had many of my friends with me. So I didn't go over, but from time to time we would write to each other. One day I even received a present from him, a pair of sandals. Sadly, David did not survive. On the last day before the liberation, the people of *Rakov* were taken to Germany by foot. His friend Silver, who was together with him and survived, told me that David was not strong enough for the exhausting march and a German shot him.

A Story about a Gold Bar

Before Josek was murdered he gave me money and a small gold bar the size of a finger. When we went to the *Selection* at the *Rinechek* on the day of the liquidation of the Small Ghetto, I was afraid to carry the bar because of a possible search. I asked Mosheh Krause, who was a member of the underground, and also an official in the *Arbeitsamt* to keep the bar with him since it was clear that he wouldn't be searched. He didn't object and took the bar. In *Hasag*, I asked him to return the bar to me, but Mosheh gave me vague answers. Then I told the story to Shimon, another friend from the underground. Shimon spoke to Krause and subsequently I finally was able to get the bar back, but Shimon told the members that the bar belonged to the underground and not to me. Josek definitely told me that the bar was from his home, but I was unable to prove it particularly as Josek had been in charge of the underground's administration. I didn't want to have hard feelings with friends, especially with some of the girls who lived in a collective with poor economic conditions. This occurred before we started to get money from outside and since I still had money, I decided to give the bar to them. Actually I didn't know what to do with it and also thought it was dangerous to keep. After the war I realized that the girls and Jatsek (Tsevi) Viernik did not know that I claimed ownership of this bar.

Shimon and Krause emigrated to the United States after the war and I saw them again only once at a party that Jatsek and Nacha

Viernik had arranged in their honor when they visited *Eretz-Yisrael*. Everybody was happy at that meeting, but I didn't get a chance to talk to them about the gold bar incident.

A Short Story about a Slap in the Face

I was lucky that among the many miracles that I experienced I was never flogged. Once I was very close, but instead of being beaten I enjoyed a not-very-strong slap in my face.

Conditions in the *Rekalibrierung* department were reasonable, work was clean, not hard and the "American" *Meister* (foreman) was a fair man. Therefore, we allowed ourselves a little more freedom, such as visiting friends at other tables, listening to gossip, etc. The night shift was a pleasure since there were no *Werkshutz* men about and the *Meister* (foreman) napped. When we had too much work we would pass boxes of cartridges without checking them, which could have been considered sabotage if we had been caught, but this didn't happen. The boxes with the checked cartridges would never stay on the table for any length of time, as the boys would immediately pass them on to the next phase.

Once, during my walk between the tables, *Meister* Nitsolek from the next department appeared, without any preliminary announcement. He was a bad, hotheaded man and his daily pleasure was to send people to be flogged in the guardroom and he often delivered the beatings. We were very afraid of him; so that when I saw him I almost froze in place. All the other girls were sitting at their places (perhaps they saw him entering) and there I stood in the middle of the hall not working. A tense silence rose around me. Scared to death I started to move toward my place. He approached me and shouted angrily: "What are you doing here? March to your place!" and slapped me in my face. I was so happy that I had been let off with only a slap that I hardly felt it. I quickly ran to my place and sat down with a great sigh of relief.

The Liberation

About two to three weeks before the liberation, the SS men arrived in *Hasag* and the situation in the camp completely changed. Every morning we were taken out, no matter what shift we worked, forced to run around the yard many times. They amused themselves by mistreating us. Then they ordered us to remove all the partitions we had made around our bunks. Instead of being in my own space, I suddenly found myself in an open big hall without any privacy. This was the lesser evil. They ordered us to paint an "H" on the backs of our coats, which I did by painting it on a piece of cloth and sewing it onto my coat. They began to pick out people and send them to an unknown destination. Tension was high as the SS men were everywhere. We were even afraid to go to the lavatory, and, of course there was no chance of meeting with friends. I felt that under these conditions I probably would not survive, but fortunately the conditions didn't last long, although at the time it felt like an eternity.

We knew that the Russians were nearing Czestochowa and that the liberation of the city was close. We didn't believe that the Germans would leave us alone, and in fact three days before the liberation they started transferring people to Germany. We were ordered to stand in lines outside the barracks and to move to the gate of the camp. People pushed to get outside because they were afraid of either being burnt together with the barracks or being shot. Things were very disorderly as some *Meisters* were gone and only the *Werkschutz* guarded us. One day many people were taken, including Danek Miska, who, I later learned, was murdered on the march to Germany.

I decided to stay at all costs where I was and convinced Susan to do the same. In the evening the rest of us were sent to the barracks. At night we couldn't sleep. We were afraid of what the Germans were preparing for us. The next morning we didn't see any *Meisters* except Nitsolek, who passed the yard quickly and disappeared. He was among the last to leave. Even though the other *Meisters* had already left, people continued to be sent to Germany. I don't remember who led this operation, but Susan and I decided to hide. We found a cellar and sat there for a few hours, until someone came and told us that a *Werkschutz* had shot a couple whom he had found hiding. We decided to leave the cellar to look and see what was happening outside. It was already late in the afternoon; there was great confusion, people running from place to place not knowing what to do. The Germans were not there anymore and a few armed guards, mainly Ukrainians, still didn't allow us to open the gates of the camp. A few fellows took the initiative, broke open the gates to the German section of the camp, entered the arms room and took rifles (I don't know if they shot any of the guards). Afterwards they forced open the second gate, which led to the street and fled to freedom. More people followed; however, Susan and I decided to stay in the camp until morning and evaluate the situation. I thought that there was no reason to be in the streets at night. It was dangerous, since nobody was waiting for us. It was difficult for me to accept that the Germans had actually left for good. Early the next morning we gathered our few belongings and slowly went out to our new freedom. We passed one gate with great tension and arrived at the main gate: it was open! We passed through it. Our dream had come true. We had survived, we were free, but I felt nothing, neither joy nor euphoria. So many times had I longed for this moment and been excited by the thought itself, but now I was indifferent and the only thought that occupied my mind was "What next?" It was hard for me to move away from the gate until Susan said; "Pola, we have to move on and find a place to live." I recovered and we started to go towards the city. On our way we met Irka and the beautiful Tsila Mintser from Lvov who joined us. Arriving at the Freedom Boulevard in town we heard calls from Polish women from the windows: " Girls, here is an empty flat, you may come in." I don't think that they called us because they were good-natured, but rather because of their fear of the Russians. The Poles always thought that Jews had great influence over the Russians, that in fact we were alike. We found an empty flat and all four of us settled down there. I don't remember details, only that there were beds, bedclothes and some utensils. There was no food in the flat, but all of us, except Susan, had some money and thus we were able to buy food. Susan and I ate together like in camp. One day Susan, a resident of Czestochowa, who knew the city, brought a sack of potatoes and we were delighted. She had found it in a cellar of a house that the Germans had abandoned.

Life after Liberation

We began to get used to life in freedom, but I will never forget the first moment outside the camp gates, the sudden awareness of being alone, no parents, no Josek, no family. Of course, intellectually I knew that this was the situation. In the ghetto and in the camp, the knowledge that we would share the same fate as our beloved and the effort not to give in to despair, to fight for survival, actually smothered the pain. Once outside the gate, walking toward freedom, this revelation caused a severe shock. Nevertheless, the instinct to live is so strong that it overrides almost everything, especially when you are young.

We started to go out, to enjoy life and to receive guests. Our flat was full of young people and we were happy to be with friends. The big question of "What next?" still remained. Susan and I had no plans at this time. I was confused and didn't know what to do with myself. Then Yehudah appeared. I knew him only superficially, as a member of *Gordonia*, he was four to five years older than me. In the Small Ghetto, the kibbutzim of *Hashomer-HaTsair* and *Gordonia* were situated in the same building and I often saw him there. I don't remember if he was a member of the kibbutz or only came to visit there. He had also been in *Hasag* and came to our barracks to visit his sister. Sometimes we exchanged a few words, but now he started to come regularly and we went out together. He told me that there was talk about leaving Poland for *Eretz-Yisrael*, but nothing certain. One day he came to take me to a "liberation party" organized by *Gordonia* members. There was a great deal of vodka and people drank a lot. I didn't drink not even wine, except at the *Pesakh Seder*, but seeing how they drank without it affecting them, I decided to have a drink too. I asked someone to pour me half a glass and I drank it all at once. I had just finished the drink when I started to feel terrible, my head went round and my eyes became hazy. I vomited suffered from diarrhea and I felt absolutely horrible. So I missed the party. When I felt a little better, Yehudah took me home and took care of me.

Meanwhile members of the underground returned from the woods and talks about going to *Eretz-Yisrael* became more definite. It was all very secretive. Only former members of the Zionist Youth organizations were involved and wanted to make *Aliyah*. It had to be kept from the Polish and Russian Authorities, so all activities and organizing was done very discretely. I didn't tell Susan about it, since she had never belonged to any youth organization. When my turn to leave for *Eretz-Yisrael* arrived, we separated, but I didn't tell her where I was going, especially since I knew that her dream was to go to America. Maybe I was wrong, but I was disciplined and responsible. Years later when we met again she told me that she felt very lonely after my departure.

During the interim period, between January 16, 1945, the day of liberation from the camp, until the end of March when I left Czestochowa, Susan and I experienced three events, one pleasurable and two unpleasant. One night we were awakened by strong blows on the door of our flat and shouts of a drunken Russian who demanded to be let in. When we didn't respond, the blows became stronger and we feared that he would break down the door. I thought I would die of fright, and we were surprised that none of the neighbors reacted, but maybe they were also too afraid. After some time the blows stopped and it became quiet. I, of course, hardly slept that night, but the next morning we found a Russian soldier sleeping in the stairwell not far from our door. He apologized for his behavior.

The second event happened when two of Susan's friends, the sisters Hanka and Bronka came to visit us, bringing a few Russian officers with them. The officers brought vodka and some food and tried to fool around with us. I was very angry with the girls who had brought them to us and not to their own flat, but I didn't know how to get rid of them. Fortunately, Yehudah appeared and said that I was his girlfriend and that we had to go. The Russians didn't make any trouble because it was their custom not to court girls with boyfriends. I went with Yehudah to his sister's and slept there. Coming back to our flat next morning I was shocked to find the whole flat full of feathers from the pillows the Russians had cut up. It turned out that the other girls had also run away from them, so in anger they cut our pillows. It was not easy to clean up the flat, nor was it easy to get new pillows.

The third event was much more pleasant. One day a group of five or six Italian youngsters arrived in the house we lived in, together with an older instructor of about 30-35 years old, also Italian. They told us that they were prisoners of war and that their instructor was supposed to bring them to some unknown place. Their story seemed a little strange, but we didn't think much of it. At first we teased them and called them "Fascists," which they, of course, denied. Later we became friendly with them, as a result of their singing. Mario, the youngest, who was about 20- 21 years old, had the voice of an opera singer. When he sang *Mama*, listeners would have tears in their eyes, as he sang with such feeling that we could feel his longing for home. Sometimes they would sing lovely sentimental Italian songs together and all the neighbors would gather to listen. We invited them to visit us a few times and offered them potato soup. We had plenty, and they were very thankful. One of them named Mauro even courted me. I managed to learn about 20 Italian words from him. After two to three weeks they left, but a few days before they left, Mauro brought me a German military blue-green overcoat. I had no idea where it came from. Later on I turned it into an overcoat for myself and it served me for many years, even in *Eretz-Yisrael*. He gave me his picture with a dedication in Italian, which I wasn't able to decipher before losing it, as well as his address in Napoli in case I happened to be there one day. It would be interesting to know what happened to these folks; maybe the Russians sent them to Siberia or to work in the mines. What a pity that the beautiful voice of this fellow should be lost. This was in February 1945, the war was still raging, but for us, of course, it was over.

I lost many other valuable items including souvenirs, which could not be replaced. There was a picture of Tosia Altman, which she gave me on one of her visits in Czestochowa with a Polish dedication, a picture of Josek and the cyanide capsule. During the year and a half in the *Hasag* camp I had watched over them like the apple of my eye. I kept them in a small parcel on my chest and when I was liberated I removed the disk with my personal number from my neck and added it to that parcel. Later I added the picture of Mauro to it and continued to keep it on my chest, but after some time I thought that I didn't need to hide it anymore and I decided to transfer it to another more convenient place. I placed the items in the pocket of the black coat, which I had in the camp. On that day the package was lost. I looked for it everywhere I went, to no avail. Maybe there was a hole in the pocket and it dropped out or somebody stole it thinking that there was money or gold in it. It has remained a mystery ever since and I have always regretted my carelessness that caused me to lose such valuable and irreplaceable souvenirs. Incidentally, I still remember the inscription on Tosia's picture. She wrote: "For Polcha Kapelushik, a souvenir, Tosia." She said that I reminded her of a girl hero in a book she had read whose nickname was *Kapelushik* (a small hat). Tosia perished in a blaze in a hideout after she participated in the uprising of the Warsaw Ghetto.

Chapter 5: The Journey to *Eretz-Yisrael*
The Start of the Journey

The probability of my getting to *Eretz-Yisrael* improved because the Jewish Agency[16] and the *Haganah*[17] established the *Brihah* (Escape) organization, whose branches were scattered all over the areas liberated from Nazi rule. The *Brihah's* goal was to organize groups of survivors for *Aliyah*, to accommodate and feed them in towns that had been chosen as transit points for eventual passage to *Eretz-Yisrael*. The *Brihah* men also provided forged documents for crossing borders from one country to another. They did tremendous work. I will elaborate upon it based upon the experience of my seven-month journey to *Eretz-Yisrael*.

Meanwhile, my relationship with Yehudah continued. I was very fond of him. We were good friends and he treated me like a princess. It is possible that I would have stayed with him forever, but he was called to Warsaw for temporary work with the leadership of *Gordonia*. He wanted me to go with him, but in Warsaw, for some reason, those in charge didn't agree.

After a short time it was my turn to start the journey. We were five girls: Rachel Beker, her sister Avivah, Halina Shmulewitz, Genia Becher and myself. Rachel was appointed leader of the group and according to her, she had chosen us. She also kept the money for our expenses. I am still in contact with her and her husband. I had not met Halina prior to this time. She was also in *Hasag*, but we hadn't met there. I knew her cousin Erna Frank-Jelin well. A few days before our journey, Halina came to me, introduced herself, and asked if I was Pola Kantor and informed

---

[16] The Jewish Agency - A public international body which worked for the *Aliyah* (immigration) and absorption of Jews in *Eretz-Yisrael*

[17] *Haganah* - Defense in Hebrew. The underground military organization in *Eretz-Yisrael* during the British rule, whose purpose was to defend the Jewish population

me that we were going on our journey together. Ever since then Halina and I, and our families have remained close friends. We meet at all family events; we traveled together by car from coast to coast in the United States and also in Europe. We maintain regular phone contact and often visit each other. Heniek (Hayim Barkani), Halina's husband is a well-known composer, who has written many beautiful songs, among them the popular *Beiti mul Golan* (My Home Opposite the Golan). They are members of the Kibbutz Sha'ar haGolan. Halina is a social worker in Tel-Aviv. For 15 years she worked in Haifa and came to visit us almost every week. They have three successful sons and seven lovely grandchildren.

In March 1945, one day after Easter, we started our journey. I put on my new coat which I had sewn from the German military overcoat, gathered my few belongings and went to the railway station. Arriving at the station I was stunned: there were crowds of people, and much tumult. Even now I don't know how we managed to push ourselves into a carriage. The trip was not easy, as we stood on our feet all the way. Nevertheless, it was not nearly as an unpleasant an experience as the trip with Mother in the open freight train when we were frozen and frightened. Now, to my great sorrow, Mother was not with me. We arrived safely in Warsaw to the transit point of the *Brihah*. The people there greeted us and welcomed us warmly, fed us and arranged lodging for us. The next morning Yehudah took us to the train to Lublin. Again there were huge crowds and much tumult, but we managed to get into a carriage. Arriving in Lublin we went to the address we had been given. Again the people of the *Brihah* took care of all our needs. Among these people I especially remember Michael Yitzhaky (Gelbtrunk) and his wife Devorah. They arrived in Israel and joined Kibbutz Tel Yits'hak. During the years that followed we maintained close relations with them.

Lublin

We stayed in Lublin for a few days and I will always remember this town as a place where something wonderful happened to me. I learned that my brother Shmulek was alive!! Here is the story. Wloclawek had become hell for the men and later for women too during the first days of the Nazi occupation. Our family decided that Father and Shemuel should escape to Russia until the danger passed. When still in Warsaw, Mother and I learned that Father had died from kidney disease and that Shmulek had been deported to somewhere in northern Russia, as punishment for registering to return home to German occupied territory. In retrospect this saved his life. Throughout the war I didn't know anything about him, but I always maintained hope that he was still alive.

One day I was told that soldiers from the Polish Army (in the name of the Polish writer Vanda Vashilewska) who had been in Russia during the war had arrived in Lublin. I thought that maybe my brother was among the group. I asked Halina to accompany me and together we went to the camp to look for him. Arriving there, we caused quite a tumult. The soldiers started to whistle, to shout and to make remarks, so we quickly ran away. I thought that if Shemuel were there he would surely recognize me. Walking in the street back from the camp, two soldiers approached us. One of them didn't take his eyes off of me. Fortunately, he was brave enough to ask me if I was Pola Cypkewicz from Wloclawek. When I told him yes, he gave me regards from my brother and he also gave me his address in Fergana, a town in Uzbekistan. It turned out that he was my brother's friend and during the last period of the war they lived in the same place in the USSR. My brother's friend had enlisted in the army, but my brother, after his unsuccessful attempt to enlist in Gen. Anders'

[18] Army, gave up. I was very excited to know that my brother was alive and as soon as I could, I wrote him a letter in which I told him that I was on my way to *Eretz-Yisrael* and I would write to him again after I had a more permanent address. Arriving in Kibbutz Beth-Zera at the end of October 1945, I sent him a second letter with my address. On April 2, 1946, I received a telegram from my brother from Fergana written in English: "Your letter received and alive well, do not send parcels, kisses your brother Shemuel Cypkewicz." (*Apropos*, when in Russia he had changed his name to Leon Tishkevitz and he kept this name in *Eretz-Yisrael*). After that we remained in close contact via letters until he came to *Eretz-Yisrael*.

Shemuel's telegram from Fergana

---

[18] Gen. Anders - A Polish General who organized an army of Polish citizens, refugees in Russia. Very few Jews managed to enlist in this army, because of Polish anti-Semitism. This army left the USSR via Iran and stopped for some time in Palestine.

Continuation of the Journey

In Lublin, the *Brihah* put us in contact with another group and from there we traveled together. They had returned from Russia and were a little older than we were. Among them were Misha Soltz and David Rubinstein who befriended us. From Lublin we continued to the Czechoslovak border, but before reaching it, we passed through Zheshuv, Krosno and Sanok in the southeastern part of Poland, not far from the Czechoslovak border. Each town was a transit point for the *Brihah*, which eased the journey tremendously. Our journey was very well organized and we traveled extremely well in spite of logistic difficulties and dangers. I don't recall many details of that journey, except that we traveled using a variety means of transportation including a cart loaded with straw, as well as by foot. It was quite a difficult adventure because the war was not yet over and many roads had been destroyed. In spite of all this, my overall memories of the trip were that it was an exciting experience.

At the last point before the Czechoslovak border, we all received forged documents from the Red Cross with Yugoslavian names. These documents enabled us to cross the border to Slovakia and then on through Hungary and on into Rumania [19]. If questioned we would have to appear as if we were Yugoslavian refugees returning home from the labor camps in Germany. I remember two quite funny episodes from this part of the journey. The train we took was full and to avoid some friendly passenger beginning a conversation with me I wound a handkerchief around my face to look like I had a toothache. Amazingly, this trick worked. The second episode was that one of my teeth actually began to ache. We joked that this had apparently happened as a punishment for my trick. I didn't know what to do, until Misha Soltz suggested

---

[19] Rumania - There were plans to send ships with illegal *Olim* (Immigrants) to *Eretz-Yisrael* from Rumanian ports in the Black Sea.

that I go and see a dentist. It was not simple to find the address of a credible Jewish dentist, but luckily we found one. What I recall vividly from my visit to the dentist was a large waiting room with comfortable armchairs. Many patients were chatting and each second word of their conversation was *Igen*, which sounded so strange to me that it made me giggle. The meaning of this word, as I found out later, was simply "yes" in Hungarian. The dentist was a very nice professional man. I seem to remember, that he refused to accept any payment because I was a refugee. The most comforting thing was that the toothache stopped. The final dental treatment was completed in Beth-Zera in *Eretz-Yisrael*. There were also other amusing events when real and legal Yugoslavians were looking for the imitators and we had to escape in order not to get caught.

Thus we traveled from place to place without any concerns and without responsibilities. Our aim was to enjoy life, which, indeed had been a gift. We were lucky to be among the first to start the journey, since there was still much disorder in Europe and borders between countries were not guarded as well as in peacetime.

Later the situation became more complicated and some people had to walk many kilometers in snow-covered mountains in order to evade border guards. A few people were caught and jailed, but eventually, all whose purpose it was to get to *Eretz-Yisrael*, reached it. This was accomplished with the assistance of the soldiers of the Jewish Brigade of the British Army, persons of high rank, as well as to ordinary *goyim* (gentiles), who competently helped the *Brihah* in its difficult task of bringing the survivors to *Eretz-Yisrael*.

Rumania

Our first stop in Rumania was in the town of Oradea-Mare. From there we went to Kluj, once the capital of Transylvania, where half of the population were Hungarians. This was an important cultural and industrial center. Between the two world wars it was also the center of Transylvania's Zionists and had a far-reaching Jewish educational network. There we stayed in the building of the former Jewish school. We were there for about two days without having enough time to tour the city, but I did manage to visit a nightclub. One evening Kazhik Rothem and Meir M. (activists in the *Brihah*) invited Rachel and me to a club. When we arrived it was almost full. At first it was nice. There was dance music and other pleasant songs and the atmosphere was good. After an hour or so the people, mainly the men, were drunk and started to throw glasses. Splinters of glass began to scatter between the tables and chairs. Seeing that the atmosphere was becoming too rowdy, we decided to leave.

I have the impression that Kluj was one of the central points of the *Brihah*, where all potential *Olim* (new immigrants to *Eretz-Yisrael*) arrived, and were then directed to Rumania and from there to other points. Until then everyone had been directed to Bucharest. We would also have gone there, but for some unknown reason, we were sent to the small town of Alba-Julia in Transylvania.

Alba-Julia

We arrived in Alba-Julia in mid April of 1945. It was a charming small town with a famous church on a hill with green meadows. Throughout history there was a church where the kings of Rumania were crowned. Before World War I this town belonged, like all Transylvania, to the Austro-Hungarian kingdom, therefore most of the population spoke Hungarian. We were surprised to find Jews in the town who had lived there throughout the war and had even been able to keep their stores. This does not mean that the Germans didn't deport Jewish youngsters from the town, but there wasn't a total extermination. We developed warm relationships with the Jewish population, especially with the young women in the town who came to see us. Sometimes we were even able to spend time together.

We stayed in a single story house, built as a great square around a yard encircled by a high fence. At one of its sides there was a high wooden gate with an opening for pedestrians. Each room had a separate door from the yard and in each room there were bunk beds for six to ten people to sleep in a room. Life was organized like in a kibbutz, with a communal kitchen and a secretariat connected to the *Brihah* whose center for us was Bucharest. There were different elected committees, such as economy, culture, work arrangements, etc. We had to take our turn at duty in the kitchen and dining room, guard the gate and clean.

It seems to me that our group was the first to arrive at this place and immediately after us more groups came including the Lithuanian group. This was an integrated group whose members spoke Yiddish and Hebrew, in contrast to those in our group who only spoke Polish. In this group there was a mild-mannered and gentle fellow named Grisha Shefer, who would go around with a stick in his hand and warn us not to speak Polish. He, of course, never used his stick; it was there only for fun. But despite his dislike of the Polish language he married Zehavah, a girl from Bialystok (Poland), who did know Hebrew, but also spoke Polish well. She passed away a few years ago in Kibbutz Eilon, where they had lived for nearly fifty years. So inevitably we turned to speaking Yiddish, full of mistakes, "breaking our teeth" to do so. Although Yiddish was not completely foreign to me, after five years of war, it was certainly not fresh in my mind. It was in this group that I met Josef Rosin, who later became my husband. Josef attracted my attention because he played his harmonica. He played all kinds of songs well, including the popular Russian songs. Without him there was no party. He was popular and was elected to the cultural committee. I liked him, but I can't say that it was love at first sight. I think that he felt the same way about me. He even dated a nice local girl, the daughter of a dentist for a short time. Josef and I were in the same group together with

Halina and her local suitor, Hanna and Yonah Rokhman, Rachel Beker, Meir Tratsevitzky (in due course he would be her husband) and others. We all went out together and spent most of our time in a *bodega* (tavern) drinking white wine diluted with soda, as was common in Rumania. After what had happened to me at the liberation party, when I became drunk on vodka I abstained from drinking vodka and at most had a sip of wine from Josef's glass. After a short time Josef and I became closer. We enjoyed taking walks and we shared many other common interests. Often we would walk uphill to the church, sit in the meadow and talk to each other about the past and sometimes even run through the meadow. One morning, I was still in bed; Josef entered the room and presented me with a small bouquet of wild flowers. He doesn't even recall this wonderful gesture, but I certainly do and it might even be at this moment that love was born at "second sight." One evening while on guard duty together at the gate, we agreed that we were indeed right for one another and so we made a commitment to spend the rest of our lives together.

Everything happened fast in comparison to normal circumstances, where a boy and a girl would meet only two or three times a week for a few hours. In our situation we were together from morning until night and time took on different dimensions. I think that the longing for a close and beloved soul mate and maybe also the wish to establish a family to make up for those we had lost, accelerated the closeness between people and between the sexes in particular. With all those events I almost forgot Yehudah, as it seemed to me that so much time had passed from the moment when I left him at the railway station in Warsaw. In fact it was only one and a half months later. One day a girl from Warsaw arrived, bringing me regards from Yehudah and a message that in two days time he would be in Alba-Julia. Although I knew that one day he would appear, I was nevertheless surprised and didn't know how to behave towards him. I rather liked him and was pleased by the way he treated me during our first days after the liberation. I believe that if we hadn't been separated maybe I would have stayed with him permanently. By this time however, I felt very connected to Josef and he had become dear to my heart. After two days Rachel entered the room where I was with Josef, and said that Yehudah had arrived and that he was looking for me. I really wanted to avoid this meeting because I didn't have the courage to tell him that I decided to remain with Josef. I asked Rachel to find some excuse for me not to see Yehudah, but she insisted that I go outside and speak to him. As I came near him, he must have sensed that something was wrong. Nevertheless, he said: "I came so that we could go to Bucharest. Please collect your things so we can leave together." When I didn't accept his proposal to join him, he was so hurt and disappointed that he didn't even give me an opportunity to explain. He left immediately, without resting from the long trip and without even saying good-bye. I felt terrible. I entered Josef's room and cried. I was sorry to have had to disappoint Yehudah, but I could not have responded in any other way. Yehudah continued on to Bucharest where he met an acquaintance from his town, whom he later married. I was glad for him and it eased my guilty conscience. (They live in a kibbutz and have three children). A few years later when we met at a yearly meeting of the former Czestochowa underground, we felt a little embarrassed, but over the years this awkwardness diminished and we were able to meet as old friends. We would also meet at other friends in the kibbutz, where he and his family lived. He passed away a few years ago.

The Wedding

On May 25, 1945, after a relationship of about five weeks, Josef and I married. It was a wedding without a rabbi because it was strictly forbidden to tell even the local Jews that Josef came from Lithuania. For security reasons the Lithuanian group posed as refugees from Poland. Rumania was then under Soviet rule, and if the authorities found out the truth they could send the refugees back to Lithuania and this, of course, was extremely dangerous for them. Years later Josef and I were married according to Jewish law in *Eretz-Yisrael*. Our friends in the kibbutz in Alba-Julia arranged a great wedding party for us. They put many tables together in the yard, making one long table covered with white sheets. Meir Tratsevitzky, who was a member of the secretariat and his friend Ephraim, who was in charge of provisions, generously prepared refreshments and drinks. Everything was going well and all were happy, until someone poured spirits into the wine and many people were drunk, including Halina. The next morning she didn't remember how she had managed to get to her room or how her eyeglasses ended up in the outhouse!

On May 9th we celebrated the end of the war. A victory parade took place in the town. Many local organizations including ours participated. After the parade there was a party in the kibbutz where Josef and two more fellows were the musicians, one played the accordion and the other a trumpet.

The good life in Alba-Julia continued as before. We were most eager for happy experiences, probably wanting to make up for the lost years in the Nazi inferno. Even the smallest event, like getting a dress from the "Joint," or a birthday was reason for celebrating.

We also celebrated my birthday on June 15th in Alba-Julia. It was then that Josef presented me with material for a gown we had both selected. It was a lovely flowery cloth that accented my suntanned face. A local dressmaker fitted and made me the dress.

Josef had some money from a ring he had sold to a local Jew, and so we bought tickets to see a guest performance of an opera being presented in a cinema in the town. The theater was terribly crowded and very hot, and believe it or not, neither of us can recall the name of the opera we watched!

Josef and I after our wedding in May 1945

One day, in the latter part of June, two somewhat drunken Russian officers, on leave in the town, appeared beside the gate and asked for girls. It turned out that the house we were living in had been a brothel before the war and the locals would send them to where we now lived. Either the locals didn't know about the changes that had taken place or they sent them to our house out of malice. If soldiers approached the gate, the guards at the kibbutz would give a signal to the girls to go into the rooms and hide. On that day all the girls hid as arranged except for Esther R., a beautiful blonde, who stayed outside her room. When the Russians saw that there were girls inside, they entered the yard, despite the guards' objections. Two strong men, who were former partisans, also tried to stop them. Then one of the Russians drew a small pistol and shot at one of the guards, injuring him slightly. As a result the Russian Military Police and high officers arrived and started to investigate who we were and what were we doing there. Our departure from Rumania was hastened by this event.

With a group of friends, Alba-Julia, June 1945

Sitting on the floor, from left: Pola Beker, Pola Rapoport, Mosheh Zinger (?), Zeldah Treger, ---.

Sitting from left: Grisha Shefer, Bolek Gevirtsman, Leizer Liudovsky, Yitzhak Vidokle, Ze'ev (Vova) Gedud, ---.

Standing from left: ---, I, Josef, Mosheh Laufgas (?), Halina Shmulevitz, Hanah Rokhman, Yonah Rokhman, Rachel Beker, David Rubinshtein, ---, ---.

From Rumania to Italy

At this time delegates from the Jewish Brigade of the British Army, stationed in Italy, arrived in Bucharest. Due to unknown circumstances, all potential *Ma'apilim* [20] would be transferred to Italy. Some people went through Yugoslavia and others, including Josef and me, went through Hungary and Austria. Up to the

---

[20] *Ma'apilim* - illegal Jewish immigrants to Palestine during the British Rule in *Eretz-Yisrael*

Hungarian border we traveled as Poles who were returning home and at the Hungarian border we received forged documents as Austrian Jews going home to Austria. The trip to Budapest may have been in a freight train in a wagon covered in a layer of cattle manure mixed with straw. The smell was awful, but we had to accept the situation as it was, although we did not do so willingly. Actually, I am not so sure that this took place on this particular journey, but that we traveled once in such a manner is certainly true.

We arrived in Budapest and to the transit point on time. I do not remember how many days we stayed in Budapest. I do remember our walk on one of the bridges over the Danube and how excited I was about the beauty of this city, in spite of the fact that it was partly in ruins. I also remember how we slept at the railway station to be sure we didn't miss the train to Graz, since the train schedule was so irregular. In Graz, we were to cross the border between the Soviet and British occupied zones, and then travel on to Italy. The train that arrived at the Budapest station was full to capacity and it was impossible to board it. Here is Josef's description about this trip, as related in his *Memoirs*. "We noticed that many compartments were occupied by only one or two Russian officers, who did not allow anybody else to enter them. For them Hungary was an enemy country. We also saw that the local population traveled by sitting on the carriages' roofs, so having no choice, we did the same traveling like this all the way to Graz. We were lucky that it did not rain during the 36-hour journey on the roof. It was amusing to see the conductor climb onto the roof in order to validate our tickets. As refugees with documents from the Red Cross, we were allowed to travel without tickets. In retrospect I would say that this journey was a very dangerous adventure because of the tunnels and the electric wires which crossed the tracks. When nearing obstacles, somebody would shout 'heads,' and we would quickly lie down instead of sitting up. Falling asleep was also very dangerous, but we looked after each other, and except for a few of our things that blew off the roof, we arrived safely in Graz."

I should add, that despite the difficulties and the danger, I enjoyed the trip. Our spirits were high and we saw humor in situations. Where would I have had the opportunity to travel on the roof of a train? For me it was really an outstanding experience, although I would certainly not choose such a venture if I had any choice. I felt as if I was in the "Wild West" without the actual shooting.

In Graz we lodged in the Hotel Weizner, which served as a transit point for the *Brihah*. At the time, it seemed like it was a luxury hotel given our frame of reference. White-coated waiters were moving around in the dining room, the tables were covered with white tablecloths and many plates and cutlery, but the food was poor and we remained hungry. On the other hand each couple received a separate room. This was very pleasant after sleeping with tens of people in the same room.

We left Graz one day later with the aim of getting to the British occupied zone. In order not to arouse suspicion we were instructed to go in pairs and to remain in visual contact with the pair ahead. The first pair knew the way; we followed and crossed the border without any problems. Halina and her companion, who were probably preoccupied and talking, chose the wrong path at some point. Instead of turning left at a particular point, they proceeded to go straight and arrived at the hut of a Soviet guard, with the whole group behind them. They were detained and sent back to the village where they started. The next day they were released and continued on their way, thanks to the friends who donated their wrist watches as bribes for the Russians. We continued on to the refugee camp established by the British Army beside the Austrian town of Villach. There we received food and a place to sleep. After a few days the British started to ask about us, who we were and where we were going. We were ordered to leave the camp secretly one by one and meet at some place down the road where a few tarpaulin covered military trucks waited for us. When we climbed onto the truck, the British soldiers from *Eretz-Yisrael* lowered the back curtain; we were told to be quiet and not to raise the curtain, in order not to arouse British suspicion. This operation was illegal of course from the British viewpoint, and we traveled for some time very anxiously, when suddenly the truck stopped. Tension rose, we didn't know what was happening outside, suddenly the curtain was raised and a man's voice said: "*Shalom Hevre* (welcome friends)." The tension broke immediately and everybody started to talk and to answer the man's questions, which consisted of questions related to his search for relatives and friends. I saw a soldier in front of me with a *Magen-David* on his sleeve, a soldier of the Brigade. This was one of the most emotional moments in my life and my eyes swelled with tears. Here, instead of a beastly German Nazi soldier, a soldier from *Eretz-Yisrael* stood in front of me one who served in the Jewish Brigade. This was an experience I absolutely knew that I would never forget.

We continued our travel on the trucks and arrived at a transit camp in the Italian Alps, near the town of Tarvisio, which had been established by the Jewish Brigade with the help of the Jewish institutions in *Eretz-Yisrael*. The place was dreamlike and beautiful and the soldiers of the Jewish Brigade, who were there on duty or who came to visit, smothered us with limitless love. They gave us their cigarettes, chocolates, uniforms etc., almost everything they received as soldiers. There were incredibly moving and touching moments. Imagine seeing soldiers meeting their brothers, or their relatives or their friends who had survived the Holocaust who they were sure had perished. It was like witnessing a happy dream that was real. One survivor met his two sons who were soldiers in the Brigade. Among the soldiers Rachel Tratsevitzky (Beker) met friends from *Hashomer-HaTsair* from Warsaw (Yisrael Gringer, Yakov Potashnik, and Yitzhak, whose family name I have forgotten). For a week we spent time with the soldiers and others taking wonderful walks in the mountains. One time we reached a high waterfall with a pond beneath. It was an unbelievable view with mountains and trees surrounding the pond. We bathed in it and romped like little children, although the water was quite cold.

One day when climbing the mountains we were caught by surprise by a strong thunderstorm. It was very frightening to be among the trees. Every thunderbolt seemed to be right above our heads. When it started to rain we ran down the mountain as quickly as possible. We were very lucky that we weren't far from the camp. Although it was a frightening experience I treasure it in my memory, like so many other memories of Tarvisio. For me, these were days of euphoria, of beauty, of something you can feel and not express in words unless you are a poet. We owed our thanks to the soldiers of the Jewish Brigade who catered to us and did everything possible to sweeten our stay there. As a result Tarvisio remains in my heart forever with love.

On July 22, 1945 we arrived in a military camp in the town of Mestre, near Venice. This was the camp of Unit 738 of the Royal Engineers, where all soldiers and officers came from *Eretz-Yisrael*. We were lodged in a big hall on the second floor of a building situated in the yard of the camp, sleeping in narrow collapsible military beds. Each bed was covered with a mosquito net for protection from the breeding mosquitoes from a smelly channel nearby. We dressed in military shirts that we received from the soldiers. Anything we didn't have the soldiers provided. There was a liaison officer from the *Merkaz Lagola* (Center for the Diaspora), also a soldier who was responsible for meeting our needs. His name was Hayim Goldenberg; we called him *Hayim Smokh Alai* (Hayim rely on me – in Hebrew), because to all our requests he would answer "*smokh.*" He was very devoted and there was nothing we needed that he didn't get, even if he had to travel long distances to find what we requested. On the outside our boys appeared as civilian workers for the army and they would often go to work together with the soldiers. Life was similar to Alba-Julia as in a kibbutz.

We are shown here, in the mountains, near Tarvisio, with soldiers of the Jewish Brigade and friends.

From left: Josef Zilberfarb, soldier, Josef, Peninah, Raya Zilberfarb, behind her a soldier, Vovke Gedud, Rachel Beker, Sima, Ya'akov Potashnik and two soldiers

Committees were elected, which took care of our daily concerns. Josef was elected to the cultural committee; they arranged *Oneg Shabbat* parties etc. There were also classes for learning Hebrew and the Bible. Dov Levin[21] was one of my teachers.

One day our friend, Yisrael Gringer, a soldier of the Brigade who was on leave came to visit us. He invited Halina and me to join him for a trip to Venice. Hearing the word "Venice," I immediately became excited as I recalled the stories my uncle had told me about the charming city on the water. I was not ready to give up this invitation, despite the fact that Josef could not join us on this day because he was busy with his work on the cultural committee.

---

[21] Dov Levin - now Professor Emeritus in History at the Hebrew University in Jerusalem and a close family friend.

On a military truck

From left: Soldier, Josef, Unknown, Unknown, Peninah

So we took the bus to Venice and after half an hour we arrived in the city of my dreams. Here she was, beautiful and unique, here was the singular San Marco square. In the middle of the square there stood the Winged Lion on a high pillar the emblem of the former Venetian Republic. In addition, there was the special San Marco church with its canopies, the Dodge Palace and the Library. Venice was built on tens of islands and with water that reaches right up to many houses on the canals. The canals make up the streets of the city and gondolas carry passengers. For pedestrians there are many arch-shaped bridges, most of them adorned with works of art. On the main channel, the Grand Canal, where the boat-buses (*Vapporetti*) cruise, there is the famous Rialto Bridge, and gondolas that primarily serve tourists.

In Mestre

From left: Raya Zilberfarb, Khayim Yaskulka, Peninah, Yisrael Gringer, and Halina Smulevitz.

Sitting: Sima, Pola Rapoport

During the pleasant walk along the main channel our eyes tried to soak in all the beauty. When we were tired Yisrael invited us to ride in a gondola. We had an accident that luckily didn't end as a disaster for me. Usually people get into the gondola on stairs at water level. Our gondolist apparently feared that somebody else might take away his tourists since there were very few tourists given that it was only about two months after the end of war. He didn't place his gondola right up to the stairs, but told us to jump into it from the quay where we were standing. This was about one meter above water. We were inexperienced and didn't know the proper way to board a gondola. To me it looked a little strange, but I remained silent like all the others. First Yisrael jumped and the gondola swung a little, but he managed to stabilize it. (By the way, the gondola was not tied to the quay.) I jumped after him and landed with one foot in the gondola and the other in the water! I attempted to regain my balance, but the gondola moved and I fell into the Grand Canal! The depth of the water was about six meters and I could not swim. I tried to get hold of the boat with my hands, but it kept moving away from me. At one moment, when my head popped up above the water, I saw many people on the quay and the gondolist and Yisrael jumping into the water. I calmed down and thought (unbelievably) that they would surely not let me drown. The gondolist jumped into the water near me and when I tried to grip his neck, he shook my hands off. At first I didn't know why and I became a little frightened until I understood that I was supposed to hold him by his hips, otherwise we would both drown. We emerged from the water completely soaked and Yisrael appeared a few minutes later. For some reason he had looked for me further away. He, of course, also came out sopping wet, his uniform and heavy military shoes dripping like a fountain. The gondolist felt guilty and offered to ride with us until we all dried off. We accepted his offer and rode for a few hours along all the navigable channels. The sun shone and it was quite pleasant, but we never completely dried out, so the gondolist took us to his home where his mother gave me an iron and I dried my flower pattern dress, the one that was made in Alba-Julia. Yisrael dried his clothes near the oven, but his shoes remained wet. When we were more or less dry we thanked the lady of the house and made our way home on foot. I had enough gondolas for a long time to come. The gondolist escorted us because without a map it was doubtful if we would found our way in the dark. We passed many narrow side streets and it was interesting to see the less romantic side of Venice, where the channels were dirty, the plaster of the houses peeling and laundry drying in the windows. Still this was Venice on the water, still something special. At the bus station we parted from the gondolist. I don't know whether Yisrael gave him some money or not. In any case he clearly didn't make a whole lot of money that day.

Our adventures on that day had not yet ended. Arriving in Mestre it was already dark when we started to walk in the direction of the camp. Suddenly we were attacked by some young Italian men. Yisrael told Halina and me to run. Halina managed to escape to the camp, but they caught me. One of them, with a knife in his hand, grasped my head and I was sure that he wanted to kill me because I was Jewish. Yisrael fought with them, and then soldiers arrived and freed me from their hands. I don't know whether the soldiers had arrived there by chance or whether somebody had alerted them to what was happening. Later we learned that all the Italians wanted to do was to cut my hair as a punishment, thinking that I was an Italian girl who had gone out with an English soldier. They did manage to cut off a few ends from my hair and to break two of Yisrael's teeth. Throughout the war years I had understood that I was in danger of being killed because I was a Jew. It never occurred to me that I could be hurt by being mistaken for an Italian. When I arrived at the camp it was quite late and Josef was already in bed. He was anxious about my late return and so he had smoked a cigarette. Suddenly I smelled smoke. Some of the cigarette ash had fallen on the mosquito net and it had started to burn. Fortunately we saw what was happening. A fire would have been one more outrageous event to end the adventures of that day. I was definitely glad to see the day come to an end as I just couldn't imagine what other horrible event could occur.

As an aside, Yisrael Gringer, our friend who took us to Venice was a member of Kibbutz Lehavoth-Habashan. He left the kibbutz, married and lived in Tivon. When he was 35 years old he died of a heart attack.

Our stay in Mestre remained a pleasant memory for us. The Jewish soldiers at the camp treated us well. They took us for trips in the surrounding areas. Thanks to them, Josef and I were in Venice many times. We went by boat to the Lido, a beautiful beach, with yellow sand and imposing hotels.

We were forced to leave this camp after about a month because British high-ranking officers started to pay too much attention to our group, questioning what girls were doing in a military camp. The *Merkaz-Lagolah* transferred us to a nice house in the village of Kiriniago, and added another youth group to ours that was from Poland. We stayed in that village for a few weeks, but I don't remember anything about it. I suppose nothing special happened there.

One day, part of the group (mainly ex-members of *Hashomer-HaTsair*), including Josef and me, were told to move to Bari, a city in southern Italy. We were taken to a railway station, where trains were leaving for Rome. In Rome we had to take another train to Bari. Josef describes this trip to Bari in his *Memoirs*: "It was extremely difficult to get onto the train to Rome. At midnight we arrived at a station, where we had to change trains to Bari. We found the correct train, but it was full to capacity. All the compartments and passages were filled with people and parcels and it seemed impossible to get inside. Then something happened which caused us to appreciate the Italian people. They started to pull us up into the train, one by one, and at the end all of us were inside with them, like sardines in a can. Sometimes it was more convenient to stand on one foot only, because there was no room for the other foot. We traveled throughout the night like this. The train was dark and all the passengers stood and sang Italian songs. It was truly an unforgettable experience." I agree with Josef that despite the hard conditions of this trip nobody complained and the mood and atmosphere were actually pleasant and even, I must say, a little romantic.

The Illegal *Aliyah* (*Ha'apalah*)

We arrived in Bari at dawn and went to an address, where we had to wait until military trucks came to take us to a remote place, amid vineyards. A transit camp for potential *Olim* called *Dror* (Freedom) had been established there. It consisted of a few barracks, a dining room, a kitchen and a lavatory. The administrators of the camp were several soldiers from *Eretz-Yisrael*, appointed by the *Merkaz Lagolah* (The Center for the Diaspora). Josef and I shared a very small living space and there we settled down, although I can't recall much about it. We passed the time in camp learning Hebrew with teachers who were graduates of the Hebrew high schools in Lithuania. There were also *Oneg Shabbat* parties with different programs, such as skits, and "broken telephone." All the skits were written and recited primarily by Josef and Barukh Shub. Usually the material was based upon daily life in the camp and about friends. Josef took an important part in those parties. His harmonica was the only musical instrument and it accompanied all singing and dancing. Overall, it was a pleasant time despite our hunger, as the food was poor so we spent our time looking for additional food. There were vineyards in the vicinity and we would pick grapes and eat as many as we could. Once some boys went to vineyards quite far away and brought back baskets and boxes full of grapes. The owner of the vineyard saw what had happened and came to complain. We were censured and from then on the vineyards were out of bounds for us, but we were lucky that he didn't complain to the local authorities, which, because of our illegal situation could have become dangerous.

We stayed in *Dror* for about a month, and on the night of October 15, 1945, covered military trucks took us to a small port near Bari. We had been told previously not to take any documents and pictures that could identify us. Josef and I handed our few pictures to an acquaintance, a soldier, and fortunately we actually received them back later on in *Eretz-Yisrael*. A small Italian fishing vessel named Petro waited for us in the port, on which four story bunks had been erected in the hold and everyone was allocated a place to lie on, 40 to 50 cm wide and high. About 180 people were crowded into that vessel, excluding the crew that included the Italian Captain and with him a *Palyam*[22] commander, a radio operator and a few Italian sailors.

We spent most of the time in the holds below because we were not allowed to climb on deck to prevent being discovered by British planes. Inside the holds it was very hot and the air smelled of vomit. Only at night were we allowed to climb onto deck to breathe fresh air, but many were seasick and didn't want to leave their beds. Leah Chertok, Hanah Rokhman and I, were all pregnant, so we had bunks near the entrance, so we could at least take a breath of air every now and then. I felt quite well, but near the island of Crete I became sick, apparently because of a raging storm that tossed our small vessel around like it was a nutshell. Water entered the vessel and filled the lower bunks with water, so that the sailors had to pump it out. At some moments I feared that we would sink, but after we passed the island the vessel stabilized. Josef felt well and he was nominated as the head butler for the limited amount of drinking water. He divided it into portions and everyone received one bottle every 24 hours. The stock of water was limited and it was critical that we save as much as possible, especially since we didn't know how long this journey would last.

After seven days we reached the shores of *Eretz-Yisrael*, but because we arrived in daylight we had to continue sailing until nightfall, in order to approach the coast in darkness to disembark. I have to mention again that this was an illegal *Aliyah* (according to the British) and the British were watching the shores.

At night we began to disembark from the vessel that was anchored quite some distance from the coast, into boats, that took us fairly close to the shore. There, in order not to get our feet wet, the boys of the *Haganah* carried us to dry land on their

---

[22] *Palyam* - the Navy unit of the *Palmakh* - the shock troops of the Haganah

shoulders. It was a funny and strange scene. Once on land we were given oranges and then started to walk, apparently to Kibbutz Shefayim, by way of an unfamiliar track. It was not easy, because after a week of swaying on the vessel, it was difficult to walk on solid earth. Everything around me was turning and swaying, and I felt like I was drunk. On our way we saw boys from the *Haganah* lying on the ground with guns in their hands to make our way safe. Arriving in the settlement we were divided up among the local inhabitants, who despite the late hour, were waiting for us. Another girl and I lodged with a very nice family.

We had a warm shower, a good meal and a bed with clean sheets, but it was difficult for me to fall asleep. Every time I closed my eyes, it seemed to me that I was still sailing and that the bed was swinging to and fro. The men, including Josef, were taken to Moshav Givath Hen, where every family took in two men. Josef and Dov Levin lodged together at the Frukhter family, where they received and enjoyed the warm hospitality of the family.

The next morning we were taken to Kibbutz Ma'anith. I have no memories of this place. Maybe it was because I was just too tired to take in anything new. After resting in Ma'anith for two days, we traveled by bus, as a *Garin*[23] of *Hashomer-HaTsair* to Kibbutz Beth-Zera in the Jordan Valley. This time I was very excited, as I now felt that I was really in *Eretz-Yisrael*, traveling the roads of the land and marveling at the inspiring view from the beautiful boulevard that led to the kibbutz. When still in the *Hasag* camp I dreamt of this day, but it was a dream I didn't believe would ever really happen. And here I was, in my chosen land, breathing its air. I was ecstatic that I had succeeded, but also sad that all my loved ones were not with me, and that many of

---

[23] *Garin* - a nucleus for establishing a new kibbutz or to strengthen the existing one

my friends with whom I had shared so much were not successful in also realizing this dream.

Beth-Zera

Beth-Zera was most welcoming, especially the veteran members of the kibbutz who were Lithuanian born. Yehudith Borokhovitz-Yaron, like Josef was from Kybartai, and she knew all of his family. She treated us especially well. We lodged in huts, three persons to a room. Josef and I were given a room, which to us looked like a palace. When I saw it I asked Josef with disbelief: "Is this room really for us?" The first impression was impressive, two beds (from the Jewish Agency) covered with nice blankets, and a closet, two or three chairs, and a small table covered with a tablecloth and on it a vase with flowers. All of this gave me a warm feeling. It was like a dream, finally a room for us. In fact, it was a small room, with partitions between one room and the next made of thin plywood. Every word from the neighbors on both sides could be heard. A few days later, we had a *Primus* in our room, as a third person in the room of a couple was called. It was our friend Rachel Zagay (later Rozner), but despite this, my enthusiasm for the room didn't abate. After a short time Rachel moved to a room for unmarried women.

On the evening we arrived, the kibbutz arranged a welcome party for us in the dining room, only I didn't attend. On our way to the party I suddenly saw an apparition that almost made me faint. I was sure I was seeing a ghost. The person I saw was to the best of my knowledge dead. I could hardly believe my eyes that this was really Avraham Zilberstein from Warsaw, a member of our kibbutz in Warsaw, Zharky, Czestochowa and the underground. I was so excited and eager to know how he survived, that instead of going to the dining room with Josef (I intended to catch up with him later), I sat down on a bench and listened to Avraham's story.

He said that on June 25th and 26th of 1943, the day of the liquidation of the Small Ghetto, one group of the underground members went to the bunker at Garncharska St. 40. Their plan was to leave through the tunnel in this bunker, to the Polish side, and then continue on to the partisans in Konitspol. Avraham was in that group. When, after crawling to the outside, he suddenly heard shots. At that moment he realized they had been betrayed and that the Germans knew all about the exit of the tunnel and were waiting for them. Since he was the last in line, he stayed put, clinging to the wall beneath the exit, so that the Germans could not see him. They also lit up the tunnel and shot into it, but fortunately Avraham was not hurt.

Outside a battle raged with unequal forces with most of the underground members killed. In that battle one German was killed and a few wounded. Only one member of the group managed to escape to Konitspol under a smoke screen from a grenade he threw. Avraham stayed in the tunnel until he was sure that the Germans had left and then went out to the Polish side and continued to Zharky, where our people were still present. They helped him to reach *Eretz-Yisrael* in 1944 when the war was still going on. It was a very difficult and dangerous journey, as he looked very Jewish and was likely to be recognized by the Poles and handed over to the Germans if captured. He endured and overcame a lot of hardships, but unfortunately I can only recall with the help of his friend Aryeh Gutkind, the key events of his journey. After Zharky he successfully made it to Bendin, where our people had contact with the Polish underground and they helped him cross the border to Slovakia. From there they helped him cross to Hungary, to Budapest and at the end to Konstanza, a port at the Black Sea. It was from there that he came by ship to *Eretz-Yisrael*. His story was so fascinating, that I didn't realize how quickly the time had passed and I never did get to the party in the dining room. Avraham passed away a few years ago in the USA. His wife Lodzha (Leah), who was a *Kasharith,* a young girl who maintained contact with the Jewish underground, and two sons, survive him.

Our life in Beth-Zera, after a week of vacation and tours of our surroundings, became routine. Josef worked at the citrus plantation and was satisfied. I, being pregnant, was put in the clothing stockroom, which didn't require any physical effort. I also was given better food, more suitable for a pregnant woman. Beth-Zera was a beautiful kibbutz with lawns, trees and flowers. Most of the people treated us sympathetically. Food was plentiful and after years of inadequate nutrition we were most appreciative of what we received. I particularly remember the yeast cakes we would eat for Shabbat breakfast, which had a taste of heaven and reminded me of my mother's cakes and of my home as a child. In spite of all this, it was difficult for me to get used to life in a kibbutz, and I felt a little lonely.

My poor knowledge of Hebrew and the lack of close friends in our group undoubtedly contributed to my feelings of loneliness. Most of the people were Josef's friends from Lithuania. What disturbed me most was the need to get up early. In the kibbutz yard beside the dining room, there was an iron pipe hanging on a cord. Each morning someone would bang with an iron bar making noises similar to a big horse bell and I would always jump up with a start because it reminded me of the camp in *Hasag*.

After two to three months we were given identity cards from the British Mandatory Government (Palestine-Israel). Afterwards we went to Tel-Aviv to visit Josef's uncle Dr. Barukh Ben-Yehudah and family. Josef's uncle was on a mission in the USA, but on his return he came to visit us at the kibbutz. Josef's cousin, attorney Avraham Ben-Yehudah with his wife Shulamith, also came to visit us. We had a very close relationship with them and we enjoyed our visits with them in Tel-Aviv, especially in the early years when we could stay in their home, before they had five children. Later on we would stay with our friends Rachel and David Levin.

With friends in Beth Zera

1- Grisha Shefer; 2-Zlatka Shefer; 3-Mira Buz; 4-Yosi Melamed;

5-Avraham Anzel; 6-Barukh Shub; 7-Dov Levin; 8-Josef;

9-Peninah; 10-Yitzhak Shpiz; 11-Pesakh Shemesh;

12-Shemuel Sherman; 13-Havivah Haitin

I liked Tel-Aviv a lot and we would go there very often. The first things I looked for in Tel-Aviv were halavah and chocolate. Finding these treats meant that the war was really over. I liked to walk in the streets, window shop and most of all to go to the theater. Despite my very poor knowledge of Hebrew, I enjoyed the show and sat with rapt attention, just as I did in my childhood. We also visited the opera and even the zoo, where I managed well without Hebrew. About this time I met Esther-Josek's sister and her husband Josef Shildhaus-Shiloh. Our first meeting was at an event at Nacha and Heniek (Tsevi) Vierniks. Later on we visited them at their home. I told them about Josek and about the *Pesakh Seder* I attended at her parents' house. We continued meeting on different occasions. They are very nice people, but now our communication is limited to exchange of greeting cards for the holidays and phone calls.

With friends in Beth Zera.

Standing from left: Unknown, Havivah Haitin, Peninah, Josef

Kneeling: Hanah and Yonah Rokhman

On Shabbat, May 11, 1946 at 4:30 AM, when we were still in Beth-Zera, our son Amikam was born in the Scottish Hospital in Tiberias, now a hotel. On Friday evening a truck driver from the kibbutz took Josef and me to the hospital, where they left me and drove back to the kibbutz. It was not easy for me to be alone especially since I didn't know the language well, in addition to this being my first delivery. It was a pity that fathers didn't remain with their wives during the hospitalization. Nevertheless, we were certainly blessed by Amikam (Ami), a lovely and healthy boy, who made me forget any of the concerns I may have had at the time. The next morning Josef arrived, after friends had awoken him with joyful shouts: " You have a son!" He brought a bouquet of flowers from the members of the kibbutz and a Hebrew book with vowels, a present from him. He then ran, of course, to see the baby through the window. Ami's birth gave us much joy and happiness.

Our first visit to Tel-Aviv, December 1945

142

At a Bar Mitzvah party at the Vierniks in Tel-Aviv

Standing from right: Tsevi (Yatsek) Viernik and Nacha Viernik, the Bar-Mitsvah boy David, Esther Kantor-Shiloh-Josek's sister (with the string of pearls)

Sitting from left: Josef Shiloh, Esther's husband, me and Josef

Outside the Kibbutz

In July 1946 our *Garin* left Beth-Zera with the aim of establishing a new settlement in Lehavoth-Habashan in the Upper Galilee. Josef decided to continue his studies at the Technion in Haifa. For two years before the war he had studied at Kovno University and we asked the kibbutz to allow us to stay there until the beginning of his studies in October. The kibbutz didn't agree and it didn't seem right to join the *Garin* temporarily.

Our wonderful friends Dinah and Yekhezkel Steinberg from Kovno came to our assistance. Yekhezkel, upon hearing that we had to leave Beth-Zera and that our apartment, which we had bought in a *Shikun* (Housing) in the outskirts of Haifa, was still not ready, invited us without any hesitation to stay with him and Dinah. When they arrived in *Eretz-Yisrael* they didn't go to a kibbutz. Instead they received a small apartment from the Jewish Agency in West Kiryath Hayim, a new quarter that was being built on the sands across the Haifa-Nahariya railway line. This was a one-room apartment where they shared a kitchen and bathroom with the residents of the opposite apartment that was similar to theirs. We managed, although it's hard to know how, to live in that room with a baby. We were supposed to stay there for only two weeks, but we were there for six weeks, because the building contractor of our apartment didn't keep his word. I am positive that these living arrangements were very inconvenient for Dinah and Yekhezkel. Both of them worked. Yekhezkel was working at *Solel-Boneh* (Pave and Build), a large construction company that belonged to the *Histadruth,* until the Technion reopened and he was able to continue his studies. Dinah worked in a shop. When they came home from work, not only did they have us, they also had the baby, who, of course, sometimes cried as all babies do. We never heard a single complaint from them. I will never forget their generosity.

There was also another situation that highlight's Yekhezkel's unique character. When we wanted to move from our apartment to another one in the *Hadar* quarter and needed money, Yekhezkel lent us 200 *Liroth* (Pounds), without any hesitation. At the time, this was quite a large amount of money. When we offered him a promissory note, he wouldn't accept it, saying that he was sure that we would return the debt. Sadly, Yekhezkel passed away when he was only 52 years old. There were not many people like him and Dinah. She died a few years ago.

I should also mention our friends Hanah and Yonah Rokhman who hosted our baby Ami, and us, for some time in their small apartment on the hill in Benei-Brak during the War of Independence. Josef was in the army and I stayed at home alone.

When we left the kibbutz, we took the two iron beds and the blankets that the kibbutz obtained for us from the Jewish Agency. We also used them when staying with Yekhezkel and Dinah. I didn't like the location of the apartment in the tenement complex from the beginning, because there were no gardens or any space where I could walk with our baby, only stairs and stairs. In order to get to the Technion in the *Hadar* quarter, Josef had to go by bus through *Halisa*, an Arab quarter, which was not very safe. I managed to stay in this housing complex only until the start of the War of Independence, when the situation in our quarter became worse. Above us was a camp of the Arab Legion. They would shoot at us from time to time. In *Halisa* the Arabs would shoot and throw grenades at the buses that passed.

Josef, Peninah and Ami at Benjamin Park in Haifa, 1947

Once they threw a grenade at the bus Josef was on as he was going to the Technion, but fortunately the grenade fell down off the roof of the bus and exploded after the bus had passed. After the experiences I lived through and endured during the war, the tension was unbearable for me, so we moved and rented a two-room apartment, a kitchen and a bathroom on Tsefat (Safad) Street No 9, on the *Hadar*, the main Jewish quarter in Haifa at that time. We sublet one of the two rooms to a tenant. Life was not easy especially when Josef enlisted in the Air Force in May 1948 and he was based in Tel-Aviv. The Technion closed down for one year at this time. I stayed alone with Ami, but I was happy that I had left the apartment in the housing complex. I would walk with Ami in Benjamin Park and on Herzl Street, and meet friends who would also come to visit me. Here the environment was reasonably quiet. When the War of Independence ended, the Technion opened up again and Josef went back to his studies. He graduated in 1950 with a degree in civil engineering. During his work at the *Tahal,* the water planning company for *Eretz-Yisrael*, he continued his studies and in 1958 earned a Master of Science degree in agricultural engineering.

On Friday, July 24, 1959, at 23:50 PM our sweet baby girl Eliyah was born in the Rambam Hospital in Haifa. We were happy to have a girl after first having a son, and on this occasion we invited our friends for a toast. The refreshments were quite modest, in keeping with customs in those days in our circle of friends. We ate sandwiches, herring and cakes.

Ami was then thirteen years and two months old. We had celebrated his Bar Mitzvah at the General Zionist's club on HaNevi'im Street, with many guests from all over the country.

In 1961 we moved into a more comfortable apartment at 41 Yotam Street on Mount Carmel.

Niva, Naor, Eliyah and Peninah in 1961 with our first car, a Jeep

We have much happiness from our two children. Ami (Amikam) graduated from the Technion with a Master of Science degree in electrical engineering and married Irith nee Oher in 1968. She is also a graduate of the Technion with a degree in biochemistry and a Master of Arts from Johannesburg University. They have a daughter Sharon, a graduate of UCLA with a degree in accounting and a son Gil, a graduate of California University in Fullerton with a degree in computer sciences.

Irith and Ami

Sharon

Gil

Eliyah finished her studies at Haifa University with a Bachelor of Arts and Master of Arts in educational psychology. She is remarried, to Zvi Toren, also a psychologist. They have a sweet daughter, Lior, today a successful student in the fourth grade in the local elementary school. From Eliyah's first marriage to Amir Veg, an industrial management engineer, she has a lovely daughter Inbar, a fine student in the eleventh grade at Nahalal High School. Ami and his family live in California in the United States; Eliyah and her family live in Israel.

Eliyah and Zvi

Inbar

Lior

My friend Susan (Sabka) during her visit to Haifa after we had not seen one another for many years

Earlier I described my separation from Susan and the reasons she didn't join me on my trip to *Eretz-Yisrael*. During the seven months of my journey we had no contact. Our contact was renewed about two years after we moved to Haifa. I still have a letter from Susan sent from Germany with a picture of her, her husband and a baby boy. From that letter, I understood that after I left Czestochowa, she managed to get to a refugee camp in Germany. There she met Ted Ostrowitz, a young Polish Jew, and they married. They intended to go to America, (in *Hasag* she had always dreamed of America and I dreamed of *Eretz-Yisrael*), but after this letter we lost contact for many years presumably because everyone was establishing a home and a family. To our delight we reconnected and renewed our friendship in the 1970's by pure chance.

One day my friend Miriam Raveh called me and suggested that we go to a worldwide meeting of former Czestochowa Jews. The occasion was the planting of a forest to honor the martyrs of that community in the Martyrs Wood in the hills of Jerusalem. Although I was not a native of that town I decided to go, hoping to meet old friends. Indeed we met people from America, Canada and elsewhere. Among them was a woman, a friend of Miriam's. Talking with her I asked if she happened to know Susan. Her answer was: "Sure, she lives not far from me." I asked for Susan's address, but she couldn't remember it. She suggested I give her my address and my phone number and she would give it to Susan.

We had no paper to write on it, so she gave me a small piece of thin paper taken from a cigarette box and on it I wrote my address using Miriam's back as my desk.

Truly, I was not sure that this note would ever get to its destination, but the unbelievable happened. After a few weeks, on a day we returned from camping, the phone rang and to my great surprise and delight it was Susan. We were very excited and happy to renew our friendship and we talked for at least half an hour. I invited her to visit us and after a short time she came to Israel. Josef and I went to the airport to welcome her. I feared that after thirty years of being apart that we would not recognize each other, but that didn't happen.

She stayed with us for two weeks and throughout her visit we talked and talked. It seemed as though time had stood still. We recounted memories and events we had experienced together and went on to describe our lives since we were last together. We have remained in contact ever since. We visited her and her family many times on our trips to see our son Ami and his family in California, and they have also visited us in Haifa.

Susan has a wonderful family. She and her husband have three successful children. Her son and one daughter, are both physicians, and her other daughter works for a TV station.

When we were in *Hasag* together, we never thought that we would be among the happy and fortunate ones to survive, much less be able to have a family, bring up children and enjoy grandchildren.

Our Wedding Anniversary Celebrations

Josef and I celebrated our golden wedding anniversary in May 1995, a happy occasion, with the family and many friends attending the celebration in the Shulamith Hotel in Haifa.

In May 2005 we celebrated our 60th wedding anniversary with family in a restaurant in Haifa.

Our immediate family on May 26, 1995

From left: Eliyah, Inbar, Irith, Ami, Peninah, Josef, Hanah, and Rivkah Shemesh

May 26, 1945 - our wedding in Alba-Julia with close friends

Standing from left: Misha Soltz, David Rubinstein, Halina Shmulevitz, Rachel Beker, Meir Tratsevitzky and Efraim--.

Sitting from left: Grisha Shefer, Peninah, Josef, and Pola Beker

Pictured are friends from Alba-Julia who were at our wedding on May 26, 1945. These are some of the same people 50 years later on May 26, 1995, in Haifa at the Shulamith Hotel

Standing: Halina Shmulevitz-Barkani, Rachel Beker-Tratsevitzky, and Meir Tratsevitzky

Sitting: Grisha Shefer, Peninah and Josef

May 26, 2005, 60 years later with family in Haifa

First row from left: Peninah, Lior, Zosha-Irith's mother, Irith, Niva, Vered, Yits'hak, Zvi

Second row: Josef, Eliyah, Hanah, Ami, and Naor

Peninah and Josef at their 60th Wedding Anniversary Party
May 26, 2005

Chapter 6: My Brother Shemuel

My dear brother Shemuel never wrote his own memoirs. Consequently, I felt the need to make his life story a part of my own memoirs. Thanks to the letters he wrote to me from Russia, Poland and Cyprus, some of which I still have, as well as the significant help from his wife Hanah, I have been able to record some of his experiences during and after the war.

In the Soviet Union

Father and Shemuel escaped to the Soviet Union at the beginning of the Nazi occupation. This was at Mother's insistence because of the unbearable terror the Germans unleashed in Wloclawek at first mainly against the men.

They arrived at the new Russian-Polish border [24], in the town of Malkinia. Crossing the border was not easy, but after waiting for a few days they managed to get to Lomzha, a town where Father had a cousin who welcomed them warmly. Father's cousin was an old man, as I recall, without any family. Unfortunately, he couldn't really help them very much. I do not recall more details about their life there, but after a short time, Father passed away from a kidney disease. I think he died in Lomzha. Shemuel, 16 years old at the time, found himself in a difficult situation, for he was alone. He asked to return to Poland especially since there were rumors that the situation at home was not so awful.

The Russians deported anyone who asked to return to Poland either to Siberia or to northern Russia. They simply put the people into freight cars and sent them to some unknown place. Their excuse for doing so was that people who wanted to go back to the German enemy could not be trusted. In retrospect one can

---

[24] After the Polish defeat in 1939, this country was divided up between Germany and Russia, thus a new border was established between Russia and German-occupied Poland.

say that this was fortunate for many of the exiles. Shemuel was sent to the Comi Autonomous Republic, to a labor camp near the capital of the Republic Siktivkar, about 500 kilometers (320 miles) south of the Arctic Circle. He told them that he had studied in a vocational school, so they sent him to work in a shipyard. He was lucky that the foreman took him under his patronage and taught him the various aspects of shipbuilding, including riveting. This was the main technique used in joining steel plates together. Years later in Israel Shemuel became the head of a section in the Israeli Shipyards. This foreman also helped him in other ways. I don't know what conditions were like in the camp apart from the bitter cold, but Shemuel didn't complain. It is a pity I didn't write down his story as he told it to me when he arrived in *Eretz-Yisrael* in 1948.

In the summer of 1941, according to the agreement between Shikorsky, the Polish Prime Minister exiled in London, and Stalin, all Polish citizens were freed from the camps, including Shemuel. Like most of the freed prisoners, he tried to get to a warmer region and so he and a few friends came to the city of Fergana in Uzbekistan. The long journey of thousands of kilometers was filled with unpleasant episodes. Once, when they slept at some station, his shoes and all the money he had earned for his work in the camp were stolen. For the rest of the trip he traveled on the roofs of the carriages. He arrived in Fergana impoverished and in poor condition. Consequently, he accepted the authorities' offer to work in a *Sovchoz*, a governmental farm. He and a few friends registered to go there on the assumption that at least there would be some food in such a place. At first everything was all right until one day the man in charge of provisions disappeared and the workers stopped receiving their daily portion of bread. They were forced to forage for food from the remains in the fields. Hungry, they decided to leave the *Sovchoz* and return to Fergana. This time Shemuel was lucky and managed to get a job in a factory, where he received food and a meager salary, but it was at least a start. After some time, the management of the factory sent him to a truck driver's course. In Russia such a course took up much time because a driver also had to be a mechanic, since there were no garages within easy reach in the vast expanses of Russia. During this period he received food and a salary. At the end of this training he was required to spend six months alongside a senior driver before he could obtain a driver's license. Thereafter, he worked as a driver in the factory, and later on he was appointed manager of a storehouse, so he was happy. At first he lived in a dwelling for bachelors and later on in a rented flat. He had a girlfriend there, but all we know about her was that she was a Jewish girl from Rumania.

On April 2, 1946, I received a telegram from him from Fergana in answer to the letter I had sent to the address I received in Lublin from his friend from the Polish army. This was the first personal message I had received from him and my delight was indescribable. Ten days later I also received a postcard from him.

With the establishment of General Anders' army, Shemuel tried to enlist and was accepted, but after they found out that he was Jewish, even though he did not look Jewish, they disqualified him. In Fergana he joined the Union of Polish Patriots that had been established by the Polish writer Vanda Vashilewska. All my letters to him were sent to the address of that union and in the name of Leon Tishkevitz. This was the name that Shemuel now used.

After he received my first letter in the autumn of 1945, he started to look for a way to get out of Russia to get to *Eretz-Yisrael*. He told me that until then, he had thought of staying in Russia. He did not like the Poles, but the possibility of going to *Eretz-Yisrael* hadn't occurred to him. He also had no idea that anyone in the family had survived. In Fergana there were rumors that no Jews remained in Poland.

In Poland

After the war the governments of Poland and Russia, the Soviet Union, signed a repatriation agreement, which allowed all citizens of those countries to return to their homeland. Shemuel left Russia as a Polish repatriate. Arriving in Poland, he first went to Wloclawek where he met our Uncle Alter, who had returned there in 1945. He was the only one from the entire family, except for us, who had survived. Shemuel went to see the house where we had lived, but he just did not have the courage to enter our flat.

In Poland, Shemuel was active in the *Brihah* and for some time administered a children's home. According to the letters he wrote to me, I can, more or less, trace his travels through Europe. He apparently left Fergana in May or June 1946 and about a month later reached Wloclawek. I received a postcard from Wloclawek dated July 10, 1946, but I don't know any details about the events of that long journey.

He stayed in Wloclawek for two weeks, lodging with our uncle, and then went to a kibbutz in the town of Swidnica. From there he sent me a postcard dated July 24, 1946.

I don't know what he did there, but I assume it was connected with the *Brihah*. After about two months he moved to Sosnowiec. From there I received two postcards dated September 16th and October 26, 1946. He wrote that he was well and that he had an important job that forced him to stay where he was for some time. He didn't explain the job to me. In Poland he went to Warsaw and Wolomin to look for more relatives, but didn't find any traces of the family.

From Sosnowiec he was sent to Bilawa, where he met Hanah, his future wife. Hanah describes her first meeting with Shemuel-Leon: "I met Leon in Bilawa near Szczecin (Shchechin) at a seminar arranged by the Zionist Youth Movement. There we primarily learned Hebrew, discussed educational problems, and our ideological way and scouting. We both learned Hebrew in different groups, because I had learned Hebrew before the war in a Hebrew *Tarbuth* school. We spoke to each other in Russian, because our Hebrew was not good enough. At the end of the seminar, which lasted for a few months, we parted ways. "

Shemuel with friends in Swidnica

The *Ha'apala* (Illegal *Aliyah*) and Cyprus

In January 1947, Shemuel arrived in Lyon, France together with a group of children from the children's home in Poland, where he had been the administrator. Most of these children were orphans and he thought that he could go to *Eretz-Yisrael* legally with them, but apparently it could not be accomplished. He left France on an illegal ship named *HaMa'apil HaAlmoni* (The Anonymous Immigrant), which was more like a bucket than a ship. He wrote to me that the journey was very difficult. The ship lurched from side to side, and three times a day it was necessary to pump out the water that seeped in. All the passenger belongings were badly damaged or lost.

The British Navy captured the ship, and after a fight with the *Olim* it was towed to Cyprus, where they arrived in February 1947. Shemuel wrote to me from Cyprus that he was reading a lot of books, learning Hebrew, but generally he was idle. In the Cyprus camp he was involved with the Zionist Youth. Hanah also arrived in Cyprus via Italy by a small illegal ship and there they met again.

Hanah, nee Weiss, was born in May 1927 in the small town of Yanuw near Pinsk in Poland, now Belarus, to a well-to-do family. There were three boys and two girls in her family and Hanah was the youngest of the five children.

According to the Soviet-German agreement of 1939, this part of Poland was occupied by the Soviets. At the beginning of the Soviet Rule the Weiss family was expelled from their large home and in June 1941 they were exiled to the Altai region. From there they moved to Kazakhstan. As a result, the whole family survived the war, except for one son who happened to be away from home. He literally disappeared without a trace.

Hanah studied in Kazakhstan, graduated high school and started to study at a teacher's seminar. After the war Hanah's elder sister married and immigrated with her husband to the United States, the remainder of the family came to *Eretz-Yisrael*.

Hanah tells: "When I arrived in Cyprus, Leon (Shemuel) was already in camp 64-65. They belonged to the Zionist Youth and they ate together in a similar manner as would be found on a kibbutz. Everyone did their own laundry, and on his visits to us, I was living with my cousins Pesia and Sender. Leon (Shemuel) was always neat and clean. He read a lot and his Hebrew had greatly improved. We spoke Russian and a little Hebrew. He was full of humor and joy and always spoke about his sister in *Eretz-Yisrael*."

In *Eretz-Yisrael*

Members of the *Haganah*, who had infiltrated into the camps as teachers, began to train the youngsters in the theory of fighting. On February 18, 1948, Shemuel arrived in Haifa after a year in Cyprus. We still lived in the housing estate, now Pe'er Street, with the Arab Legion above and the Arab *Halisa* quarter below us. There had already been incidents with the Arabs. I can't recall how I learned that he had arrived, but I do remember that I worried that he might lose his way and wander into the Arab quarter. Josef went to look for him and found him in our quarter. It is difficult for me to describe our meeting for we were both very excited. We hadn't seen each other for about eight years, but to us it seemed like an eternity. The abominations of those years, the fight for survival, the absolute separation from each other and from the family made me feel as though I was living in another era, as though the years before the war didn't exist at all, as though they were only a dream. The meeting with Shemuel brought me back home to my former life and created a connection with those times. We spoke only in general terms about our experiences during the war, and for some reason we didn't offer details and I wonder why. To this day I still don't have a clear answer. Perhaps we were not yet able to relive the terrible events.

After a short time Shemuel started to work at the shipyard of Grinspan and Kirstein in Haifa bay. He continued to keep in touch with Hanah, who was still in Cyprus, through letters and small parcels he sent her. The impression Hanah had from his letters was that he had acclimated well to the country, and his friends envied him because he had a place to live with his sister and brother-in- law.

In the War of Independence, in May 1948, Shemuel was mobilized into a unit of mainly new *Olim*, who didn't know Hebrew, didn't understand the verbal orders and hardly knew how to use guns. Eliyahu Rishpaz, Shemuel's friend, recalls that after a short period of training, they were sent to conquer Latrun from the Arab Legion. Latrun was an important place in the battle for Jerusalem. It was a bloody massacre and many of our soldiers were killed, including survivors of the *Holocaust* who hadn't even managed to see anything of the country. These soldiers were conscripted straight off the ship. I had no idea that Shemuel was taking part in the Latrun battle. Even so, I worried and blamed myself for his coming here at exactly this time. I know that people will say that I was egotistical, but I don't care. He was my brother, the only person, except for an uncle, who hadn't perished in the war and I just couldn't lose him. We were lucky in that he was placed in a unit of heavy mortars and not with the attacking infantry. As a result he survived the hell at Latrun. I understand that the situation was critical, but I cannot forgive those who sent the survivors of the *Holocaust* to an almost certain death directly from the ship where they had landed. These poor people were never afforded the opportunity to establish new families in place of those destroyed.

After Latrun Shemuel was transferred to the shipyard of the Navy, where he served for some time as a *Samal* in the permanent army. Later on he continued to work there as a civilian.

Hanah recalls: "When I arrived here in May 1948, he came to visit me in the new *Olim* camp in Hadera. In March 1951, we married and rented a flat on Pinath Yalag St. No 3 in Haifa. He had many friends, among them Eliyahu Rishpaz and Yurek Shemer, who would visit us often to play chess and cards. Later we moved to Kiryath Eliezer, where we bought a flat and while living there, Naor (January 30, 1956) and later Niva (August 12, 1958) were born."

I remember that Hanah and Shemuel's wedding was held in Hanah's parents' home in Ramlah. Josef, five-year old Ami, and I went by bus to that joyful event. Josef already owned a camera and he took pictures of the beautiful newlyweds. It was a very modest wedding and only attended by family members.

This was during the *tzena* (period of austerity) in the country and food was sold only with special ration cards.

Second from left: Shemuel as a *Samal* in the Navy

Hanah continues her story: "In 1956 he started to work in the Israeli Shipyards where he changed his name from Leon to the Hebrew name Aryeh. He advanced steadily at work, where he learned technical drawing and became a foreman. He was not mobilized during the Six Day War in 1967, but conscripted to the shipyards. In that year we moved to a larger and more spacious flat in Kiryath Motzkin, which was closer to his work. In due course he was sent to Iran for a few weeks and several times to Eilath for ship repairs. In 1969 he was sent to the Lursen shipyards in Germany for half a year to qualify for building motor gunboats for the navy. On his return he was appointed section boss (No. 14). He did well at work and in 1981 was awarded, The Distinguished Worker Citation, on behalf of The Israel General Workers Organization. There was an article in the *Ma'ariv* newspaper on November 17, 1981 describing this event. From 1982 to 1983 he was offered the position of branch director, which he refused saying that his English was not good enough. In 1985 there were work force reductions in the shipyard and he retired on an early pension. He enjoyed retirement. He was a member of the Country Club in Kiryath Motzkin. He learned to play bridge in the club and sometimes played it at home. He enjoyed life until he became very ill in 1989 and in July 1992 he passed away."

The pensioners committee of the shipyard and the pensioners' organization of *Solel-Boneh* planted trees in his memory in the *Solel-Boneh* woods in Modi'in.

He was a gentle and polite man. Even when he was very ill he tried as hard as possible not to burden others. He felt terrible that he could not take care of himself. I was with him in the hospital almost every day from afternoon until evening. Once he said to me: "Look what has become of me. I'm like a helpless child." When Josef and Eliyah came to visit him, he would always smile at them and ask how they felt, in spite of his own poor physical condition and pain.

The above article, published in the *Ma'ariv* newspaper on November 17, 1981, announced Shemuel's being awarded the "Distinguished Worker" award.

Hanah and Shemuel

Shemuel, Hanah and her Parents, Ramlah 1951

Shemuel was honest, sincere and industrious and very devoted to his family. He worked hard to assure their well being. He was also a devoted brother, and I knew that I could always rely on him. He was generous, not only to his children and grandchildren, but also to others. Upon returning from a trip abroad he always brought presents to my family too. All the nice suits Ami received as a child were from Uncle Shemuel and Aunt Hanah.

He and Hanah, who was a beautiful and industrious woman, had a lovely family and a warm home. They raised two successful and devoted children, Naor (Ori), an economist with a Master of Arts in business management and Niva, a building and electronics technician. They are both married; Naor is married to Daniela, nee Talmi, from Kibbutz Dan. She is a clinical psychologist and they have three wonderful daughters Shahar, Meirav and Oriyan. Niva married Yits'hak Saban, an electronics engineer. They too have three lovely daughters Adi, Mor and Dana.

Shemuel was so happy when they were all born and it is a pity that he could not live to see them grow up. Although the effects of the war on his life were not easy, they didn't change his character. He remained sincere and faithful just as I remember him from our childhood. Let his memory be blessed!

Our families were very close. We would usually meet every two weeks, alternating at their flat and ours. Shemuel's children, Eliyah and Niva, almost the same age as my children, were close friends and spent most summer vacations together. When Ami was a little child and we had to go somewhere, he would stay with Shemuel and Hanah. We are still constantly in touch and celebrate their granddaughters' birthdays together. I am sure that Ami and Eliyah also have warm feelings for Shemuel and Hanah. Hanah is a lovely and optimistic woman despite the troubles she experienced.

Shemuel (Aryeh) in Germany where he studied building motor gunboats for the Israeli Navy

Niva and Yits'hak

Naor and his second wife Vered

The Liquidation of the Wloclawek Jewish Community

After Mother and I left Wloclawek at the beginning of December 1939, the deportations of Jews from the town continued. On December 15, 1939 people were deported to Wloshchowa-Zamoshch and on February 15th to Tarnow. These deportations took place at night and the deportees were allowed to take only a small parcel of clothes with them. Most of those who were deported later perished in the death camps. After the deportations, only about 4,000 Jews from the original 10,000 who had been in the town at the beginning of the war, remained in Wloclawek. At the end of October 1940, a ghetto was established in the run down district near the Jewish cemetery, where streets were not paved and there was no electricity. One thousand Poles were evacuated from those outskirts and they moved to the Jewish flats in town in order to make room for the Jews. On November 9, 1940 a barbed wire fence that was guarded by SS men enclosed the ghetto. Inside the ghetto a Jewish Police unit was established to maintain order.

Early on the Poles and Germans were allowed to enter the ghetto and the Jews were able to exchange clothing for food. After a short while hunger began to overwhelm the ghetto population as the Jews had no more clothes to exchange for food. Only tailors and shoemakers who worked in German plants were able to obtain food for their work. At their initiative a public kitchen was established in the ghetto that prepared free warm meals for tens of people. Despite these inhumane conditions the youth of all the Zionist organizations, the *Bund* and the Communists arranged cultural activity in the Room of Purification[25] of the cemetery, where lectures and amateur shows were held.

A few days after the German invasion of the Soviet Union, on June 22, 1941, hundreds of men were sent from the ghetto to

---

[25] Room of Purification - for washing the dead before burial.

forced labor in Poznan. On November 6, 1941 the Germans closed the ghetto completely and the situation became desperate. Jews who were caught trying to obtain food outside were shot, and several Poles who tried to deliver some food to their Jewish friends were also shot. At the end of 1941 the Germans completely destroyed the Jewish cemetery and smashed all the gravestones except for those made of marble and those they removed.

The deportation

In the spring of 1942 the Germans started to liquidate the ghetto, and about 400 men, aged 14 to 50 were transferred to labor camps in the Poznan area. Most of them died of diseases and hunger, and the survivors were sent to Auschwitz in 1943.

On April 27, 1942, the ghetto was liquidated. The Germans put the remaining 1,000 Jews, mostly old women and children, on trucks and transferred them to the death camp in Chelmno. This was the first camp where the Germans murdered Jews by asphyxiating them with the exhaust gases of special trucks built for that purpose.

Thus, the vibrant Jewish community of Wloclawek, so full of good deeds, was exterminated by the evil deeds of the Germans.

In 2001, the Wloclawek Municipality erected a monument in memory of the murdered Jewish community. On June 15, 2001 an impressive inauguration ceremony of the monument was held with former Wloclawek Jews from different countries participating in the ceremony. The mayor of the town and a guard of honor of the Polish army were also included in the ceremony.

The monument for the martyrs in Wloclawek and vicinity at the Holon cemetery

(Picture taken and provided by Gershon Kuchinsky)

The Polish and Hebrew inscriptions read: "In this place the Germans established a ghetto in which Wloclawek Jews were concentrated. In June 1942 the ghetto was liquidated and the Jews were sent to death camps."

EPILOGUE
A Return Visit to Poland

In the summer of 1994 Josef and I with a group of people visited Poland. The first town we visited was Warsaw. I looked for something familiar, but sadly could not find anything. The part of Nalevky St. where the kibbutz had been situated, house number 23, didn't exist and in its place there was a garden. The streets of the ghetto, except for their names, also looked very different to me. I presumed that the reason was that the Poles had rebuilt the city after its destruction and only the old city had been restored to its previous appearance.

The rebuilt old city of Warsaw

Behind the monument is a railway station where the Jews
were taken from the Warsaw ghetto to Treblinka

מכאן אותם הובילו
בשנים 1942-1943
תחילה
בדרך של עינוי וסבל
אל אושוויץ 300000-כ יהודים
מגטו וארשה
אל
מחנות-ההשמדה הנאציים

The plaque inside the monument reads: "From here in the
years 1941-1943 during the German rule more than 300,000
Jews from the Warsaw ghetto were transported by a way of
pain and torments to the Nazi death camps."

Monument to the rebels at the top of their main bunker on Mila Street in the Warsaw ghetto

Close up view of the monument to the rebels at the top of their main bunker on Mila Street in the Warsaw ghetto as pictured on the previous page.

Monument in memory of the Warsaw ghetto fighters

My granddaughter Inbar stands in front of the section of the ghetto wall that serves as an important reminder of what happened there. She read two excerpts from my book to students visiting Warsaw.

We visited most of the death camps and although I had witnessed the means that the Germans used to exterminate people, I still couldn't fathom the fact that human beings who called themselves civilized committed all those atrocities. How could they be so cruel and so inhumane?

One of the most terrible places we visited was the Treblinka death camp. About 40,000 to 50,000 Jews from the Czestochowa ghetto, 300,000 Jews including 150,000 children from the Warsaw ghetto, and hundreds of thousands of Jews from other communities and other countries were murdered there.

This terrible campaign began in July 1942 and lasted until August 8, 1943 when the prisoners revolted and escaped from the camp shooting some of the German and Ukrainian guards and burned down the entire camp. It was never reconstructed. Sadly, only a few of the rebels managed to survive their ordeal.

In Treblinka, the Polish government established an impressive monument in memory of the victims who were murdered there. Hundreds of stones were placed in the area, each one representing a destroyed Jewish community.

The front of the monument in Treblinka

A stone beside the monument with the inscription in seven languages: "NEVER AGAIN"

The stone at Treblinka in memory of the Czestochowa Jewish community

Wloclawek

After the war ended I had no desire to visit my hometown. All its pleasant memories had been obliterated and in their place remained the terrible picture of the Nazi occupied town and their *Actions* against the Jews. In recent years I began to long to see the street and the house I had lived in, the streets I used to walk, the beautiful park and the other places that had meant so much to me. Josef and I left the group for one day and hired a taxi and went to Wloclawek; it truly was the main reason for our coming to Poland. I was excited and filled with expectations without really knowing why. Maybe I was hoping to relive my childhood and adolescence, but I also feared that I might awaken memories of the atrocities I had witnessed at the time of the German occupation. None of this happened. Instead I felt like a stranger in an almost strange city. My memories just didn't coincide with the current reality. The entrance to the city had changed and a new neighborhood had been built there with white dwellings. It was impossible to walk along the Third of May Street where I had strolled with my friends because of road construction. The shops that were once owned by Jews seemed unfamiliar to me. The Old Market square, through which I would return home, had changed, as many of the houses and shops had been removed and instead there was a garden overlooking the Wisla river. Only when passing the fish shop and the pharmacy where I used to buy pills for Mother when she was ill, did I feel a gnawing in my heart. I continued on to the street where I had lived, but it looked narrower to me and neglected. The small house, through which I would enter the yard and from it go to the big red brick house where we had lived, was also in disrepair with peeling plaster. The gate didn't exist anymore. I entered the yard and saw an empty space. What had once been my home, was now just a small piece of wall, and my heart ached. I continued on to the promenade along the Wisla River. It remained as beautiful as ever, although a little different because new places were added where one could sit. We went along the promenade by taxi to the little square where the band of the 14th regiment used to play. It didn't exist anymore. Only my tree stood in its old place and that stirred me.

Except for the names of the streets I didn't recognize any of the houses where my friends had lived, nor the Jewish public buildings. It was only the church that stood in the vicinity that reminded me how dangerous it was to pass by it on Sundays.

I left Wloclawek with a feeling of a lost opportunity, a feeling that I had not prepared myself well enough for the visit. Interestingly I was left with a strong longing to visit it again, despite the pain of knowing that Jews no longer lived there. I would have liked to have been able to just sit there, not for two hours, but to stay for two or three days and stroll the streets by foot. I came away disillusioned and saddened. This was not "my" Wloclawek anymore. Nevertheless, it is still the city where I was born and grew up. It was, however, difficult for me to put my feelings into words for the city was both familiar and strange and attractive yet unwelcoming all at the same time.

Third of May Street in 1994

Peninah near the new steel bridge

Peninah standing near the small section of her ruined house

Small entrance house to the yard of Peninah's home

The Square of Freedom with the monument of the Unknown Soldier

Concluding Thoughts

I managed to survive this horrible period of time by being lucky and using my ingenuity. I am also extremely grateful for the help of good people whom I will never forget.

I am happy that Josef and I have been able to provide our children and their children good lives here in *our own State of Israel,* the land of our dreams. We have enabled them to live a Jewish life. It is extremely important to me that my family knows my story so that they can appreciate where they came from. It is a story that my current and future descendants should have access to, so that they too can appreciate what it was like to be a Jew in the 1930s and 1940s, when a cruel enemy wanted to destroy us. It is now the responsibility of current and future generations to preserve what I, and so many others fought for, our freedom from persecution and our right to live an ordinary life without harm just because we are Jews.

I also expanded my memoirs into a book format so that those who are not our direct descendents can also understand the history of the Jewish people who lived through such a horrendous time, It is my hope that by reading this memoir told from a personal perspective that people will be able to appreciate the richness of the Jewish heritage that was so brutally destroyed throughout Europe. May we, and all people throughout the world, never defile human beings again and take away their spirit to survive.

* 9 7 8 0 9 7 6 4 7 5 9 9 6 *